GW00707872

WALK ON,
WALK ON

A Play

WILLIS HALL

SAMUEL   FRENCH

LONDON

NEW YORK   TORONTO   SYDNEY   HOLLYWOOD

MADE AND PRINTED IN GREAT BRITAIN BY
LATIMER TREND & COMPANY LTD PLYMOUTH

MADE IN ENGLAND

GW77982

WALK ON, WALK ON

First presented at the Liverpool Playhouse on November 26th, 1975, with the following cast of characters:

Gillian Dugdale	Anne Stallybrass
Randolph Preston	Philip Guard
Bernie Gant	Glyn Owen
Frankie Womersley	David Beckett
Terence Bullivant	Alan Rothwell
Harry Nicholls	Michael Cotterill
Douglas Leadbetter	Robin Wentworth
Jacqueline Gant	Pamela Blackwood

The play directed by Leslie Lawton
Setting by Billy Meall

The action of the play takes place in the General Office of a Third Division football club

ACT I   Two o'clock on a Saturday afternoon towards the end of the football season

ACT II   An hour and three-quarters later

Time—the present

ACT I

The first-floor general office of a Third Division Football League club

There is a large window in the rear wall that looks down over the pitch. A door leads downstairs to ground level and to the pitch, dressing-rooms, etc. A second door leads to the board-room, other smaller offices, the directors' box, etc. Although, going by a circuitous route, it is possible to go out through either door and return by the other

It is two o'clock on a Saturday afternoon—an hour before kick-off—towards the end of the football season. Gillian Dugdale, who runs the office, is sitting at her desk, typing. Bernie Gant, the club's manager, who is in his late forties, is gazing out through the window that overlooks the ground. He has his back to us, and stands silent and motionless, his hands deep in his overcoat pockets. Randolph Preston, an old-age pensioner who "helps out" in the office, is on the telephone. He is waiting for Gillian to stop typing. He manages to catch her eye at last

Randolph (*into the telephone*) Yes, so the question is, Nelson, can I leave it to your tender mercies to fix up then—without you making your usual mullocks of it? . . . Do we have to go into details now? We've got an extremely serious kick-off in an hour's time . . . I mean, that's entirely up to your discretion, but if it was me, going on past experience, I'd ring them up and order a common or garden wreath, preferably in the shape of a football, with an amber and black ribbon round it. Tell them who it's for, they've made them up for us on umpteen occasions . . . I don't know, Nelson, put what you like on the card—stick "Get Well Soon" on it if you want, except it would hardly be appropriate if they're burying the feller. How about "From all his close friends and associates at the City"? . . . That depends on how many close friends and associates you can rustle up. Say twenty pence a-piece and reckon on fifty and your hovering in the region of a tenner, then think of a number and double it, I leave it entirely to you . . . (*He puts down the phone*) That'll cost you twenty pence, Gillian—you come under the category of close friend and associate.

Gillian Who's dead?

Randolph I'm not a hundred per cent certain, to be brutally honest. One of the doyens of the Supporters' Club. I have a strong suspicion it was that stiffish-built chap with the bald head.

Gillian I don't think I knew him.

Randolph You would do if you saw him. You'd know him well enough to come under the category of associate if not close friend.

The phone rings on Gillian's desk, and she answers it

Gillian City ground. . . . Yes, it is on, kick-off three o'clock. Good afternoon.

Randolph Mind you, if it is who I think it is, the bald head wouldn't mean a lot to you. Because he seldom took his hat off. You'd know him better as the stiffish-built chap in the trilby hat.

Gillian Do you want the money now?

Randolph It would save me the embarrassment of having to come back to you later.

Gillian picks up her handbag but, before she can open it, the telephone rings again

Gillian City ground. . . . Yes, it is, kick-off at three o'clock . . . good afternoon. (*She puts down the phone and gives Randolph her donation*)

Randolph I wish I could think of his name for you, Gillian. He was always standing in the corner of the Supporters' Club—feeding the fruit machine and swearing under his breath.

Gillian There's always somebody dropping dead.

Randolph That's life, Gillian. You know what they say: "That's football". (*He glances across at Bernie's back*) I won't bother him now. Shall I go and see if she's got the kettle on in the tea-bar?

Gillian I'm not all that bothered.

Randolph I am. I could just manage a cup.

Randolph goes out, through the door leading downstairs

Bernie turns from the window

Bernie He's pulled his last jackpot then, out of the Supporters' Club one-armed bandit, the feller with the bald head.

Gillian You mean the feller with the trilby hat.

Bernie Ask not for whom the three bells toll—or the plums or the cherries.

Gillian It's all right for some—keeping your back turned. It's cost me twenty pence.

Bernie He'll get me after the final whistle if not before. Where's the sun decided to hide itself? Isn't it bloody marvellous? Saturday afternoon again—it's been scorching down all week.

Gillian It isn't raining, is it?

Bernie It's doing its best to. It'll take at least a thousand off the gate. An hour before the kick-off, you can set your watch by it. Do you want to know what I'm beginning to think? Because we're in the Third Division, God sends us Third Division weather.

Gillian The rain it raineth on the just and on the unjust too.

Bernie Don't you believe it. Haven't you ever noticed when you've watched the telly? The weather's always great for the big stuff. The sun shines down regardless on the First Division. But just take notice when they televise a Second or Third Division match—there's always a dark cloud up there, hovering. It's always us poor struggling sods that get bad weather. It's God, you know—he does it on purpose.

Gillian What does he do to the Fourth Division?

Bernie Ask me again at a quarter to five tonight. I might be able to tell you—we could be in it.

Gillian It's not certain though, is it? Even if we lose today? We still stand a chance of missing relegation?

Bernie There's a mathematical possibility, as the football reporting Einstein on the local rag is ever-anxious to inform us. If we manage to snatch a nil-nil draw and two other bottom of the table clubs get thirteen apiece knocked in against them. In that unlikely event, we'd stand every chance of missing the drop. Otherwise, we have to win today—or count on miracles. I've given up expecting miracles me, in this game. He hasn't got time for miracles these days God—he's far too busy buggering up the weather.

The phone rings. Gillian picks it up. Bernie turns back to the window

Gillian City ground. . . . Yes, it is, three o'clock kick-off . . . 'Bye.

She puts down the phone and looks at Bernie, but he has turned back to the window. Gillian goes back to her typing

Randolph bustles in, carrying three cups of tea on a battered tea-tray

Randolph I am right, aren't I? It is you that doesn't take sugar?

Gillian nods

What about his lordship?

Gillian One-and-a-half teaspoons.

Randolph He'll have to settle for two. I've just had a hell of a shock. I walks out of here, I walks into the Supporters' Club, I only nearly walks straight into him. He's standing there as large as life, trilby hat, bald head, bunging five p. pieces into the fruit machine like a maniac. It isn't him at all that's popped his clogs. It's a totally different chap altogether. I'm buggered if I know *who* it is—it could be anybody. It's got me worried.

Over the above, Bernie turns back from the window

I'm just saying, Mr Gant, there's somebody snuffed it from the Supporters' Club.

Bernie I'm not surprised, the way we've been playing—I've not been feeling too well myself lately.

Randolph It'll come. It'll come. We'll get it together. It's happened before and it'll happen again. It goes in cycles. I've been supporting this club for over forty years—I've been in this office for over twenty. I've seen us go up into the Second Division twice, and then come down two times again. Triumph and tragedy. You know what they say: "That's football". But we continue to continue. We survive. We have to. We only need to snatch two points today and the position will look entirely different. Confidence, Mr Gant. We've had a lot worse teams than this one now and beaten relegation. I've seen six managers come and go at this club since the war—and that's not counting you, Mr Gant, that isn't. It's what it's all about, is confidence. Don't you worry. Shall I pop down to the visitors' dressing-room and ask their manager for his team changes as per the printed programme?

Bernie I should give it half an hour, Randolph. I know that crafty sod of old—he won't announce anything until the last minute—until he has to.

Randolph It's no bother. You never know, he might have them ready. I'll tell you what's just occurred to me. Do you know that old chap with the Kaiser Bill moustache that rides about on a motor-bike pillion? It could be him that's kicked the bucket.

Randolph goes out downstairs

Bernie "I've seen six managers come and go not counting you—don't worry"—I never know whether he's taking the piss or as thick as two planks. (*He glances out of the window*) Hello! They're starting early, aren't they? There's three of our hooligans and three of their hooligans on the terrace behind the far goal kicking lumps out of each other.

Gillian Is that unusual?

Bernie It is at ten past two inside the ground. They usually skirmish in the streets until a quarter to—shouting abuse and warming up by kicking in a few shop windows. They must be taking this one seriously.

Gillian Aren't we all?

Bernie I'm sweating on it, that's for sure. My whole bloody future's resting on it. Two kids, one at school and one at college, a club-house I'm living in—if I have to leave that house I've got nowhere, literally—I've got no contract with this club I can fall back on. If I get the bullet here I don't go away with a penny-piece, I'm knackered.

Gillian A wife and two kids.

Bernie Didn't I say that?

Gillian No, just two kids you said.

Bernie Same difference. I was taking Joyce as read.

Gillian You always do—I've always found that difficult.

Bernie That's a subject I'd rather not pursue, forty-five minutes before a kick-off. Jesus God, will you look at them! They just stand there and kick each other. When I was a player I used to be on that pitch for ninety minutes and go home with less bruises than the spectators these days. Where's it going to end, I wonder? Bugger the lot of them. Thanks for last night, by the way—I enjoyed myself.

Gillian Good.

Bernie Are we all right for tonight again?

Gillian I'm still thinking about it.

Bernie Be like that. Do you happen to know if the chairman's arrived yet?

Gillian Not to my knowledge. Unless he's come in the other way and gone straight to the board-room.

Bernie You haven't heard anything, I don't suppose, from anyone?

Gillian Heard anything about what?

Bernie You know what I mean, Gillian? Have you heard anything on the grape-vine about the directors' get-together last night?

Gillian Forgive my ignorance, but I hadn't even heard that this club had a grape-vine.

Bernie You usually know what's in the wind.

Gillian Not about last night. I was otherwise engaged myself last night.

The phone rings, she picks it up

City ground. Yes, three o'clock kick-off . . . Don't mention it. (*She puts the phone down*) I wonder *why* they ring up? Every time we have a home fixture? They must *know* it's on. There's posters all over town, it's in all the papers. If it rained all night, you could understand it. Do you know what I think? I think they do it to show off. They're standing in a pub. They say to their mates, "I'll just ring the club up to make sure the game's on." Do you know what else I think? I think that the ones who do ring up never come to the match. They go back to the bar. "Yes," they say, "it is on." And, if they're lucky, some-body's got a round in while they've been away, and they go on drinking. All afternoon. (*She changes the subject without a pause*) I shouldn't worry about last night, it wasn't a board meeting—just a few of the directors getting together.

Bernie Yes, but why? You can't tell me they were socializing. Half the buggers can't stand the sight of the other buggers. Of course I worry— I'm a football manager—I'm a professional—they're all bloody ama-teurs, yet my job stands or falls by that lot.

Gillian I think they were round at Terence Bullivant's house, weren't they?

Bernie Yes, and you can't tell me that the club secretary invited them in to lash them up on light ales and gin and tons and little bowls of tatie crisps and peanuts. That will be the day, the day Bullivant treats anybody. He's got a rubber waistcoat—when he gets near a bar he bounces off it. They were round at his place wheeling and bloody dealing. Was Harry Nicholls there, I wonder?

Gillian I don't know, Bernie! I don't ask what the chairman gets up to when he isn't here—all I ask is that he pays me the same courtesy and keeps his nose out of my leisure-time activities.

The telephone rings, she picks it up

Yes, the game is on and the kick-off is at three o'clock as advertised in the local—— Hello . . . Oh, hello . . . Very well, thank you . . . Yes, he's here at this minute, I'll put him on. It's for you—your wife.

Bernie (*taking the phone*) Hello, Joycey? . . . Yes, of course, if you want to, you should have said . . . No, not the slightest trouble—two in the directors' box, I'll leave them on the main gate for you . . . Thanks, I have a feeling we're going to need it . . . Look, I might have to do a bit of flying around afterwards—you know—the usual ducking, dodg-ing, diving and darting. Talking to the press and so on—so I'll see you when I can . . . Righto, Joycey . . . Thanks.

Gillian She's coming to the match?

Bernie We've got Jacqueline home from college for the week-end. She fancied the game, I think. They've decided to come together. Can I leave the tickets for you to arrange?

Gillian Of course. I'll do them straight away.

A pause, then Randolph bustles in again

Randolph He's an ignorant bugger, their manager—a real dyed-in-the-wool ignorant bugger.

Bernie I told you that before you set off.

Randolph I knocks on the dressing-room door, there's this dogsbody answers it. I says, "Would you kindly ask your manager if he has any team changes or is he as per printed programme?" He says, "Just a minute, I'll ask him." He slams the door in my face. I hang on a couple of minutes, the door opens. It's him this time, their manager, Porter. I says, "Excuse me, Mr Porter, do you think I might have your team changes or are you as per printed programme?" He says, "Who the buggery are you?" I says, "I'm a City Official." He says, "I didn't think you were the referee." He says, "What time is it?" I says, "It's nearly two-fifteen, Mr Porter, and could I have your team changes or do I take it that you are as per printed programme?" He says, "You're a bit quick off the mark, aren't you? Come back at half-past." Then *he* slams the door in my face. I'm just walking away when he opens it again. "Hey," he says, "if you're a City Official, I've got a very serious complaint to make." I says, "What's that, Mr Porter?" He says, "Your bloody tea's as cold as clap." And he slams the door in my face again.

Bernie I did warn you.

Over Randolph's speech, Gillian takes two tickets from a cupboard, seals them in an envelope and addresses the envelope

Gillian Could you get these tickets to the main gate, Randolph, the next time you go out?

Bernie You haven't caught sight of the chairman, by any chance, Randolph, while you've been out on your travels?

Randolph No. But he's about somewhere. His Jaguar motor-car's parked up on the car-park.

Bernie I'll have a look round for him. I'll be down the board-room end, if wanted.

Bernie moves towards the door to the office

Randolph Mr Gant, before you dive off—have you got a second?

Bernie For you, Randolph, anything.

Randolph Our team changes. For the loudspeaker and the referee—or are we as per printed programme?

Bernie (*after some thought*) Yes. No. There's a bit of a doubt about Roger Gilligan—he's still carrying that pull he got in training. I have to see the physio before I make a firm decision. Do I have to tell you now, Randolph? Ask me again at half-past two, would you?

Bernie goes out to the office

Randolph "tut-tuts" with frustration. Gillian goes back to her typing. Randolph picks up his tea and sips at it

Randolph I'll say this much for Porter, he was right about the tea—it is clap cold. It's bloody freezing. (*He looks out of the window*) What's been happening down there, then?
Gillian In the ground? Is it the hooligans? There was some trouble a couple of minutes since.
Randolph The bobbies have got them. There's four of them—bobbies—carrying off a couple of yobbos, kicking and struggling.

The telephone rings, Gillian answers it

Gillian Yes—it is. Three o'clock kick-off. . . . Not at all, good afternoon.

Gillian puts the phone down. There is a knock on the door leading to the ground

Come in.

One of the players, Frankie Womersley, enters

Randolph dismisses Frankie with a glance, and then speaks to Gillian

Randolph (*looking on a table*) You haven't seen a pile of programmes, have you? I've left the board-room programmes somewhere, and I'm buggered if I can remember where I've put them down.

Gillian shakes her head, then turns to Frankie

Gillian Can I help you, Frankie?
Frankie Is he up this end, is he?

Randolph pauses in his search for programmes and frowns

Randolph Who's "he" supposed to be when he's at home?
Frankie Plonker. Thingy. The boss man. King Dick.
Randolph If you're looking for Mr Gant, Frankie, he's got a name. Say, Mr Gant. Or ask for the manager. And, no, he isn't up this end, he's down the other end, where you ought to be.

Randolph continues his search for the elusive programmes

Frankie Have I missed him, then? Has he gone down to the dressing-room already?
Randolph Not yet. But he will be going down to the dressing-room, at some stage in the proceedings. Very presently.
Frankie Terrific. I'll hang on here and catch him then, before he does.
Randolph (*to Gillian, puzzled*) I haven't taken them down earlier on, have

I? You haven't seen me walk out of here with a stack of programmes in my hand? I'd know if I had.

Gillian shakes her head

Terence Bullivant, the club secretary, in his forties, enters from "outside" and crosses the general office

Terence Afternoon.

Randolph Good afternoon, Mr Bullivant. Today's the day, eh? The big decider. We need two points, of vital necessity.

Terence pauses at the door to the offices and favours Randolph with a cold, polite smile. He turns to Gillian

Terence Is the chairman in his office or in the board-room?

Gillian He's not in his office, he might be in the board-room. Mr Gant went down to look for him a couple of minutes ago.

Randolph He's definitely about somewhere, Mr Bullivant. His Jaguar motor-car's parked up on the car-park.

Terence (*to Frankie*) Shouldn't you be in the dressing-room?

Frankie I'm waiting to see the boss.

Terence What about?

Frankie A personal matter.

Terence What kind of personal matter?

Frankie A private one.

Frankie stares at Terence, insolently. Terence holds his gaze, coldly, and then turns away. Frankie moves to a filing cabinet and leans his elbow on a pile of programmes

Terence I shall be in my office for the next five or ten minutes, Gillian, if the chairman puts in an appearance.

Randolph Righty-ho, Mr Bullivant.

Terence goes out to the office

Frankie "Righty-ho, Mr Club Secretary." You want to chalk your name across the soles of your shoes, Randolph.

Randolph What on earth for?

Frankie In case we have to identify you when you disappear completely up the club secretary's arse.

Randolph You want to be careful, young man. I've seen players transfer-listed at this club, before now, for being cheeky to club officials—and better players than you as well.

Frankie, who has been purposely leaning his elbow on the stack of programmes on top of the filing cabinet, suddenly "discovers" them

Frankie Are these programmes anybody's or are they going spare?

Randolph They're my programmes! I've been searching high and low for them!

Frankie What do you want twenty programmes for, Randolph? Are you working a swindle on the lucky programme number?

Randolph Give them here.

Frankie (*picking up a pen*) Shall I autograph them for you? "Yours in sport, Frankie Womersley?"

Randolph Don't you mark them programmes. They're the directors' programmes for the board-room. Don't you put ink-marks on them. Give.

Frankie hands Randolph the programmes but keeps one back

Randolph And that one.

Frankie (*hanging on to the programme*) You don't begrudge me a programme, do you, Randolph, surely to Christ? I mean, stone me—you know what I mean? I know the club's hard up and the chairman's only got a building firm, a haulage business, a rent-a-tractor fiddle and a villa in Alicante to fall back on, but surely you can afford to spare one single solitary programme for a member of the playing staff?

Randolph There *are* programmes for the playing staff, put out specially in the dressing-room.

Frankie (*challenging Randolph's authority*) I happen to want this one.

Randolph (*sourly, beaten*) Bloody have it then, Womersley. I haven't got time to play about—we've got a match on. (*He turns to Gillian*) I'll get these programmes round to the board-room before the directors start asking for them.

Gillian Can you drop those tickets, they're for Mrs Gant, at the main gate on your way back?

Randolph picks up the envelope from the desk

Randolph Certainly. I've got to call in at the away team dressing-room again.

Randolph goes out

Gillian gets on with her work. Frankie studies his programme, one eye on Gillian. At last, he speaks to himself, but loud enough for her to overhear

Frankie Dearie me! Stuff me gently with an iron crow-bar. I'm not only down as substitute, they've even spelt my name wrong.

Gillian, ignoring Frankie, goes on typing. The telephone rings on her desk

(*Unnecessarily*) Telephone.

Gillian (*into the telephone*) City ground. . . . Yes, it is, three o'clock kick-off. (*She puts the phone down and goes back to work, aware of Frankie's eyes on her*)

Terence Bullivant enters from his office, picks up a file and is about to return but pauses

Terence Has anybody done anything about ordering a coach for Monday to take us up to that reserve team fixture?

Gillian It's booked here at the ground for two o'clock.

Terence Speaking of two o'clock—it's a quarter past turned. Are you supposed to be in the squad today, Womersley, or aren't you?

Frankie I'm only named as substitute in the programme.

Terence That's not an answer to my question. Didn't Gilligan get a pull yesterday in training?

Frankie shrugs diffidently

Hasn't Mr Gant been back yet?

Gillian He's probably caught up with the chairman somewhere, Mr Bullivant.

Terence goes out, slamming the door

The telephone rings

Frankie Telephone.

Gillian (*into the telephone*) City ground. . . . Yes, it is. Three o'clock . . . Good afternoon. (*She puts down the phone and returns to work*)

Frankie Tell them it's cancelled, I would. (*No response*) Tell them the ground's waterlogged because we've had a burst pipe in the players' bog and we're waiting for a plumber. (*No response*) Tell them the water's rising steadily, the corner flags are all submerged, and the board of directors are building an ark in the middle of the pitch in the hope of divine intervention against relegation. (*No response*) Has anybody ever told you that you've got a very sexy way of saying nothing?

Gillian Has anybody ever told you to piss off, Frankie?

Frankie Yes—six referees and three linesmen.

Gillian Congratulations then, you're about to make it into double figures. Piss off, Frankie.

Frankie Oh, that's charming, that is, isn't it? What a great turn of phrase. Highly delightful. Lucid. That's the sort of language I expect to get in the players' bath from that big hairy-arsed centre-back.

Gillian Do you want something, Frankie?

Frankie Depends what's on offer?

Gillian You know what I mean. I mean now, in here? It's twenty past two, it's Saturday afternoon, it's match day. I've got a lot of work to do.

Frankie Now, why does everybody keep reminding me? I've already had it from Randolph and the secretary. I *know* it's match day, love. I read it on the posters outside the ground; it's written up on the notice-board; it's plastered right across the programme: Saturday the seventeenth—so it's got to be today has that, hasn't it? The dressing-room pongs rotten of pre-match nervous sweat and bloody liniment. Great. Terrific. The secretary will be knocking back the scotches and scoffing pork pie slices with his cronies in the board-room. There's Randolph scooting about like a decrepit school monitor with cups of tea for the referee and directors' programmes, and loving every minute. There's the chairman ducking and diving somewhere, hiding, probably locked inside a bog, shitting himself in case we go down to the Fourth Division. That's what they call total involvement. Stupendous. I'm supposed to be wearing number twelve on my back and spending ninety minutes wearing out a track-suit bottom on the substitute's bench.

At which point, Randolph scuttles in, flustered

Randolph He still hasn't got his team changes, their manager. I wash my hands of him. (*To Frankie*) Oh, and I shall be requiring twenty pence from you, and all the other players. You can tell 'em, for a wreath. Just as soon as I work out who it is that's dead. (*To Gillian*) We're wrong again. It isn't that senior citizen who rides pillion. He's standing by the tea-hut in his crash-helmet and leathers. (*He picks up a jug*) I've got the tea to organize now for the match officials. Wouldn't you know it—one of the linesmen's on a diet. How do you get three teas in one jug—one without sugar?

Randolph goes out again

Frankie That's what I mean. Involvement. What turns you on?
Gillian Not a lot, Frankie, these days—not as far as football goes.
Frankie What? Only football managers?
Gillian Shall we drop that subject?
Frankie I don't mind. How about giving it a break tonight, then? What about you and me?
Gillian You and me?
Frankie Could be. What do you fancy? An Italian dinner down the Romana? A bottle of Italian plonk and spaghetti and chips and that? Or would you rather go into the Imperial and scrub round dinner, just cane a few Bacardis?
Gillian No, thanks.
Frankie Why not? I'll pick you up after the match in the players' bar.
Gillian You won't.
Frankie Why not?
Gillian Because I've no wish to, Frankie. And I'm already meeting someone after the game.
Frankie That's a bit of a turn-up, isn't it? I thought his wife was coming to the match?
Gillian I said, leave that out.
Frankie Tomorrow night, then. I'm easy.
Gillian I'm afraid I'm not—no.
Frankie Have it your way, darling—make it Monday.
Gillian I'm not interested. How many more times?
Frankie For what reason?
Gillian *Reason?* You're talking to *me*—not one of the sixteen-year-old scrubbers from the Supporters' Club. They might leave their knickers

behind the season ticket holders' stand after two shandies on Bingo
nights—I don't. I haven't got Frankie Womersley embroidered all over
a black and amber scarf. Bloody hell, Frankie, how old are you?

Frankie Twenty-two, what's that got to do with it?

Gillian You're not even twenty-one until November.

Frankie You've done your homework then? You're keeping tabs on me.

Gillian I type out the players' pen-pictures for the programmes. According
to the programme notes, Frankie, you were still playing for North Lane
Road Comprehensive School fourteen-year-old-and-unders six years
ago. Let's leave my age out of it, but I've been running this office for
twelve years. You're not in my league, Frankie Womersley—as far as
I'm concerned, you're still playing for the Juniors.

Frankie And what league does Bernie Gant qualify for, in your associa-
tion? The Chelsea Pensioners' eleven? Or do you give him a run out in
the evenings as a charity fixture?

Gillian If you were big enough and old enough and man enough I would
hit you hard across the mouth. Get out of my office.

Frankie I'm waiting to see the manager.

*At which point, Bernie Gant returns, senses the atmosphere, and addresses
Frankie coldly*

Bernie What are you doing up here?

Frankie Waiting to see you, boss.

Bernie In the general office? On a Saturday afternoon? At twenty past
two? I'm on my way now to the dressing-room to talk to the team. I'll
see you there.

Frankie I wanted a personal word in private first. That's why I came up
here.

Bernie considers the request for several seconds, and then turns to Gillian

Bernie Anybody been in here, asking for me?

Gillian The secretary's in his office, he's wondering where the chairman's
got to.

*Loudspeakers dotted about the ground start up, and the strains of pop music
filter into the main office through the window left open by Randolph*

Bernie The chairman's in the board-room. (*To Frankie*) Won't it wait, lad,
till after the game?

Frankie shakes his head, slowly and emphatically

All right. Do you mind, Gillian?

Gillian I'll use the chairman's office.

Gillian picks up some work and goes out

Bernie closes the window

Bernie Yes?

Frankie I'm not satisfied.

Bernie You're—not—what?

Frankie I'm not satisfied.

Bernie You've got the bloody gall to stand there and tell me you're not satisfied? I'm managing a club that's third from bottom of the Third Division, as of this immediate moment. We have to win this one—a bloody draw's no use—and we're up against a club this afternoon that's chasing promotion, hasn't lost a match for three months, and is riding on a crest a mile high. I'm struggling to field eleven dead-beat walking wounded. You're not satisfied? Well, I'll tell you this, lad, I'm not exactly laughing my cobblers off either. Don't you bloody stroll in here forty minutes before the off and tell me you're not satisfied. Get down that dressing-room.

Frankie Why? What for? I'm only named as sub. Have you looked inside the programme? They've even got me down as Womersley with two emms.

Bernie I couldn't give a bugger, lad, if they've got you down as Pillock with a capital "P". Because that's what you are in my estimation. Now, get yourself into that dressing-room and get yourself stripped off and get yourself into that number nine shirt and stop bloody arsing about before I lose my temper.

Frankie I'm not playing.

Bernie Of course you're playing. Roger Gilligan's not fit. You're in the team.

Frankie I'm not playing.

Bernie You don't tell me whether you're playing or not, Womersley, I tell you.

Frankie I'm not playing.

Bernie Jesus bloody Christ, you complain when I leave you out and you complain when I put you in!

Frankie I'm sick of being a sodding yo-yo, in and out—I'm tooled off with reserve team football.

Bernie Bloody grow up, Womersley, you've not been good enough for a regular first team place, and well you know it, lad. You're that bad, Womersley—I'm running a struggling Third Division side, three places off the bottom, and you're not good enough for my first team squad. You—and you were earmarked for the England Under-Twenty-Threes two years ago. You're in today because Gilligan's out, that's why, not because you've earned a place.

Frankie I'm not in today at all. I'm not playing.

Bernie What went sour in you, Frankie? All too easy was it? Too much crumpet too much pop? You tell me, because I don't know. When you came to this club you were eighteen years old, and every time you touched the ball the sun glowed from your arse, lad. It did. It glowed. It used to light up that park. I used to sit on that bench and feel the warmth.

Frankie I want away, don't I? I want a transfer from the club.

Bernie I know what you want, Womersley, and it's not a transfer, lad, and nothing would give me greater pleasure than to administer the punishment. You want a transfer? For how much? What do you think I should put you on the market for? Shall I tell you what you're worth, Womersley, in hard cash? Bugger all. Naff all. How dare you come to me at this time on a Saturday—this Saturday—this particular Saturday of all Saturdays—and start dictating what you want and what you're going to do? How bloody dare you? I could screw you, Womersley, you realize that, don't you? I could screw you up hill and down dale. I *could* put you on the transfer list. I could ask just that little bit too much for you, so that nobody would want to know—I could have you buggering around in my combination side until it broke your bloody heart. I needn't do that even. I could put you on a free transfer, and still make the word so bad on you inside the League that not another club would touch you. I could put you on a free, Womersley, and arrange it so that you wouldn't get picked as a spongeman for a manky Sunday morning side. I could do that to you and it would give me nothing but endless pleasure, Womersley.

Randolph enters from the office side, assesses the situation and ducks straight out again

Shall I surprise you, Womersley? Shall I tell you what I am going to do? I'm going to give you an opportunity to redeem yourself. Because that's how big I am. There are two games left this season. Two. Today and a reserve team match on Monday. You'll play in both those games— not because I want you in my side, but because I've got no choice— and you're going to turn it on. Twice. That's all. Not for me, not for the club, but for the person that you love the most—you. And if you do that, Womersley—and only if—you can have your transfer. You can go. Wherever you like. And no hard feelings. And do you know why? Not because I'll be doing you a favour, I'll be doing it for me. Because I'll be overcome, over the moon, double-delighted to see you go. Now go get changed.

Womersley goes out

Bernie moves to the window, opens it, and looks down. Again we hear the sound of pop music from the loudspeakers around the ground. Bernie turns back into the room

Randolph!

Randolph enters

You can have my team changes now. You can take them to the referee and then to Maurice on the speakers.

Bernie closes the window

Randolph He hasn't got any, Porter, he's as per printed programme, after all the fuss and palaver he created.

Terence Bullivant enters from his office, returning the file he took out earlier

Bernie scribbles inside a programme as he continues

Bernie Gilligan out; Womersley in at number nine; Olliphant in as sub.

Bernie hands the programme to Randolph who moves to the door, then pauses

Randolph The other side's as per printed programme, Mr Bullivant.

Randolph goes out

Terence You've decided to play Womersley, then?

Bernie I didn't have much choice. Gilligan's not fit. I did think of putting Sweetman in the back four, moving Lancaster up front, and leaving Womersley out as sub.

Terence You mean you actually considered pushing Lancaster up as a striker?

Bernie It did cross my mind as a possible solution. He's had some experience. He used to play up front before he came to us for his County Youth side.

Terence Did he really? I never knew that.

Bernie He was the leading goal-scorer one season.

Terence You live and learn, don't you?

Bernie But I decided to take the chance on Womersley in the finish—he's got the ability to do it for us.

Terence If he'll make the effort.

Bernie I've just given him another bollocking.

Terence Did he listen?

Bernie He made polite noises. He went through the motions.

Terence It's about all he ever does, is that—off the field or on it.

Bernie He's got more natural ability than the rest of them put together, if he frames himself, has Frankie Womersley.

Terence Plus all the natural-born ability of a dedicated, tried and tested, natural-born, idle bugger.

Bernie I've got to take the chance with him. We either win today or spend next season in the Fourth Division. He wouldn't want that any less than any of us.

Terence Does he know what he does want?

Bernie A transfer—he's just asked for one.

Terence Would any other club stand for him?

Bernie shrugs

Bernie They might—on his previous past record.

Terence Let's get shut of him, then, I would.

Bernie I didn't say they'd pay money for him. He's got it. That's the aggravating thing about Frankie Womersley. Whatever it is, he's got it and the others haven't. And they'll run their legs off for me, and he won't stir a muscle. But he's bloody got it—it's maddening. If anybody can turn it on today up front, it's Womersley, if only the young sod would apply himself. It's instant death or bloody glory this afternoon. He knows the situation.

Terence Let's hope so. (*Meaningly*) But it's not his head that's on the chopping-block, is it? Have you any other problems, teamwise?

Bernie How many do you want to know? Gogan's still feeling his left peg from his cartilage operation; my keeper's running a temperature and should by rights be in his wanking chariot; Duncan McLeish was studded last week and has got more bandages than Tutankhamen. Since we lost by five in the cup match against Leeds, the defence is playing with about as much confidence as I'd have giving eight strokes to Jack Nicklaus; we've completely lost it midfield, God knows for what reasons and up front we can't knock goals in, apart from which, the situation's not too gloomy. Overall, in answer to your question, I'd say we've no more problems than usual.

Terence It sounds as if the manager's not exactly oozing confidence.

Bernie No. He's being realistic. He's being honest. I don't show it in the dressing-room. You asked me.

Terence (*glancing at his watch*) Just over thirty minutes to kick-off.

Harry Nicholls, the club chairman, enters. He is in his middle forties, he has come from the board-room where he has been entertaining the visiting directors, and he is holding a glass of scotch

Harry Good afternoon, Terence.

Terence Good afternoon, Mr Chairman.

Harry (*giving Bernie a quick smile*) I've said good afternoon to you once already, Bernard. Are we going to do it?

Bernie We're going to do our level best.

Harry Nicholls goes to the window and looks up at the sky

Harry The weather seems to be on the upgrade. We might even see the sun by kick-off.

Terence It'll be too late to help us with the gate though. We could have done with the sun an hour since.

Harry opens the window and once again, we hear the sound of pop music from the ground's loudspeaker system. Harry glances down at the crowd

Harry I don't know so much, I don't know so much. There must be knocking on for a thousand down there now. That's quite encouraging for two-thirty.

Terence It's more than we'd get for a Fourth Division fixture.

At which point, Randolph enters

Harry While there's life there's hope. We're not dead yet, are we? What's your opinion, Randolph?

Randolph Good afternoon, Mr Nicholls. I think we'll do it, personally speaking. I think the lads are going to surprise a lot of people this afternoon, the press included. Speaking of being dead though, if you'll excuse me changing the subject, Mr Nicholls, I'm going to have to come for twenty pence to you.

Harry I beg your pardon?

Randolph We suffered a very sad bereavement in the Supporters' Club, hadn't anybody told you?

Bernie If you'll excuse me, I'd better get down to the dressing-room.

Harry Wish them all luck from me.

Bernie I will.

Harry Tell them the board's counting on them.

Bernie Of course.

Bernie goes out down the stairs

The pop song comes to an end on the loudspeakers. We hear the voice of the middle-aged amateur disc jockey who runs the club's P.A. system. His opening words though, are drowned by Randolph

Randolph I was just saying, Mr Nicholls. Have you heard about the very sad demise of one of the leading lights in the Supporters' Club?

Harry Nicholls holds up a finger to indicate that he is trying to listen to the announcement

Voice Good afternoon, everybody, and welcome once again to Endersby Road. A couple of team changes for you first of all. Our visitors this afternoon are as the printed programme, but there are two alterations to the home team. Instead of Gilligan at number nine, read Womersley. And instead of Womersley at twelve, read Olliphant.

The above announcement is greeted with a groan of disappointment by the home spectators in the ground

I'll just repeat that: at number nine, Frankie Womersley; number twelve, in place of Womersley, Olliphant. Those are the only changes. And now I've been asked to play a request record for one of our most dedicated female fans whose eighteenth birthday it is tomorrow . . .

Over the above announcement, Harry Nicholls closes the window

Harry He's taking the gamble on Womersley then?

Terence So it would appear.

Harry The crowd don't like it too much.

Terence Can you blame them? I can't say I'm wildly hysterical at the thought myself.

Harry I suppose he didn't have much option, considering the injury situation. We're struggling to put any sort of side out.

Terence There are other avenues.

Harry Such as?

Terence Well, for instance—what would be wrong with him putting Sweetman in the back four and moving Lancaster up front, leaving Womersley as sub?

Harry Norman Lancaster can't play up front.

Terence He was a front runner before we got him.

Harry Are you sure?

Terence Positive. He played for his County Youth team as a striker.

Harry Norman Lancaster?

Terence Oh yes. I never forget a name on a programme. I remember seeing him some years ago. I also seem to remember him being the leading goal-scorer one particular season.

Harry Have you told Bernie this?

Terence Have you ever tried telling Bernie Gant anything? You can't tell him—he kids on he knows it all already.

Harry becomes aware that Randolph is not only in the room but is also listening avidly

Harry He likes to make his own decisions and we've always allowed him that prerogative. And if he thinks Womersley can do it for us . . . (*Then, changing the subject*) What was it you were saying, Randolph, earlier on, about somebody leaving us?

Randolph Very sad, Mr Nicholls. One of the oldest stalwarts of the Supporters' Club.

Harry Which one?

Randolph We haven't quite placed him yet. I've got him in my mind's eye, but I just can't manage to put a face on him. But it came as a shock, I don't mind telling you.

Harry Yes, it would have done.

Terence Are there many in the board-room? Have the away team brought a lot down with them?

Harry Don't they always, this lot? They're more like a swarm of locusts than a board of directors. I wouldn't care if they looked after us when we went up there—but look what happened when we played them early on in the season. There was four of us in their board-room. There was you, there was me, there was Stephen and there was David Gideon-Smith. And what did they lay on for us? We had a cup of luke-warm tea before the kick-off—and even that was a case of, "I'm sorry, we're a bit short of milk"—we had a cup of watery Bovril at half-time—mine hadn't even been stirred, it was all stuck to the bottom of the cup—at full-time they laid on fish-paste sandwiches, a bowl of cheese and onion crisps and a plate of bloody ginger biscuits. The bottle of Scotch went round so fast I hardly saw the label, let alone sniffed the contents. Then it was handshakes all round, the best of British luck, and we were on the coach and on the motorway by five-fifteen. If they call that foot-ball hospitality, I think I'll start supporting cricket. And that was after they'd beaten us by three goals to nil. God help the teams that go up there and snatch two points!

Randolph It's the same in their Supporters' Clubs bar, Mr Nicholls. *And* they don't look after the players: no soap in the dressing-room, no toilet paper in the players' karsey—there isn't—we have to take a roll of bog paper up there with us on the coach.

Harry Thank God this'll be the last time we meet them this season, that's all I say. ·

Terence It could be the last time for several seasons—if they beat us today and gain promotion to the Second, and we get relegated to the Fourth.

Harry That's something else you have to contend with: that bloated bloody chairman of theirs, boasting and crowing and extracting the urine. I've come out of the board-room to keep out of his way.

Terence Duggie Leadbetter?

Harry Douglas Leadbetter. Self-styled family butcher extraordinaire. He's got a chain of butcher's shops as long as a string of sausages. He's about as thick-skinned as one of his own black puddings. Do me a favour, Randolph.

Randolph Certainly, Mr Nicholls.

Harry Take this glass down to the board-room, would you? Knock discreetly on the door and get someone to quietly slip a refill in it, without disclosing my whereabouts. Will you join me in one, Terence?

Terence You know my habits by now—never before a match.

Randolph takes Harry's glass and moves to the door

Randolph Scotch and soda, is it, Mr Nicholls?

Harry Tell him not to drown it, would you?

Randolph Over and out.

Randolph goes out

Harry opens the window again. Again we hear the music from the loud-speakers, but this time it is backed by the roar of the crowd

Harry They are flocking in, you know. I'll bet that crowd has doubled in the last five minutes. We could end up today with the biggest gate all season.

Terence Relegation stuff. The morbid buggers have come to gloat.

Harry Not at all. Look down there. You'd think they'd come to watch a cup-final, not a bottom of the table side. Scarves, banners, woolly hats—they've come to cheer us on.

Terence Yes, but for how long?

Harry You're too cynical, Terence.

Terence Am I? They'll be our supporters at the kick-off, yes. It'll be choruses of "We'll support you evermore" at three o'clock, and we'll never have to walk alone. But if we're a goal down with ten minutes to go, they'll have given up that lot, they'll be trudging out of the ground in droves with their heads down and faces as long as the league tables. Calling us rotten. That's how long evermore lasts in soccer terms. That ground will be deserted at twenty to five, with the exception of the ones that stay behind to moan and jeer.

The music stops on the loudspeakers and we can now hear the chanting of the crowd

Harry They're the ones that pay the money at the turnstiles—they're entitled to an opinion, I suppose.

Terence Listen to them now, like bloody sheep. They don't have opinions of their own. If we go down to the Fourth Division, they'll want a scapegoat, that's all. You've had a couple of seasons here, I've been in football all my working life, I *know*. Things haven't changed all that much in sport since they queued up for the Coliseum in Rome—if things go wrong it's thumbs down and sling somebody to the lions. Mad-headed buggers. (*He closes the window*) We only need to lose today, and there'll be hundreds of those loyal fans of yours gathered underneath the directors' box, yelling and screaming for the manager's dismissal.

Harry The lunatic fringe, perhaps.

Terence For the most part—not entirely. It isn't just the fans, you know. Perhaps it's not for me to say, but there's more than one voice in the board-room that thinks it's time we had a change—manager-wise.

Harry Who?

Terence That's *definitely* not for me to say, is it?

Harry You don't have to—I've a fair idea who at least a couple of them are. Mad-headed buggers aren't entirely restricted to the terraces. We get them in the board-room too.

Terence But as far as the club's concerned, you'd like things to remain as they are?

Harry I would as far as the manager goes. It's not his fault we've been plagued with injuries all season. It's not been his fault that there's not been any cash to spare. Yes—I am behind the manager. Aren't you?

Terence I'm only the club secretary. I'm a paid official, that's all. I don't have a vote.

Harry You have an opinion.

Terence Yes.

Harry And?

Terence Permission to speak my mind? Within these four walls?

Harry Of course.

Terence You could be taking a short-sighted view. It is just possible that the voices in the board-room that want Gant out, belong to those men who are one hundred per cent behind you.

Harry I'm not entirely with you.

Terence You've had two seasons with the club, as chairman, Bernie Gant has been here for three almost. Relatively speaking, you're both new brooms. When Gantie first arrived, we were shaping up like promotion candidates for Division Two, today we look doomed for Division Four. There could be some who think that one of the new brooms isn't doing its share of sweeping clean. You did say I could speak my mind.

Harry Is all that fact or guesswork?

Terence (*making a see-saw motion with one hand*) I keep an ear to the ground.

Harry Are you saying you've heard that there are some directors on the board that want me out?

Terence No. Now you're putting words into my mouth. All I'm saying is, the wrong result and the fans will be queuing up, like I told you, underneath the directors' box, shouting and howling for somebody to go. If they don't get the manager's head on a plate, they could start screaming for somebody else's.

Harry We don't run this club to suit the mad-headed buggers on the terraces.

Terence They're the ones that pay the money at the turnstiles—your words, Mr Nicholls, not mine. They'll want somebody to carry the can. If the board passes a vote of confidence in the manager, somebody's head will have to roll. And it would seem a pity to antagonize your biggest supporters by defending a manager that they want out.

Harry I'm not defending him. I just happen to think he's good at his job.

Terence Can I really speak my mind?

Harry By all means—do

Terence Just this—abilities apart—can I refer briefly to his personal life?

Harry No. Don't. I'm not interested, Terence. I don't wish to know. I take the view that his personal private life is his private and personal concern. O.K.?

Terence All right. Agreed—so do I. Always provided that he keeps it personal and private.

Harry Terence . . .

Terence No, don't interrupt me, just a minute—if he wants to run around with spare crumpet, as a married man, that's his affair. I don't mind. I mean, if it does him some good to run a dodgy bird on the side, eases his tensions, all well and good. I don't want to interfere. Good luck to him. Always provided he keeps it on the side, on the touch-line of his life. But when he starts to do his pulling inside the club, has it off with a bird who's had more pricks than a double-sided dart board, makes himself a laughing stock to everybody from the boot-boy down, then it's my business too. If Bernie Gant wants to shit on his own doorstep, he's a bloody fool to himself, that's all. But when he does it at this club, it's not only his own doorstep he's shitting on—it's also mine. And I'll be buggered if I'm going to stand back and watch him drag this club not only down to the Fourth Division, but also into the dirt.

Harry (*after a pause*) It has turned nice all of a sudden. The sun's come out. If we are going to go down to the Fourth, we couldn't have chosen a better day to get the chop, there's that about it.

Terence I apologize whole-heartedly if I've overstepped the mark.

Harry Mind you, I don't think we will go down—I've got this feeling in my gut.

Terence Let's hope we don't.

Harry Do you know that sensation when you wake up some Saturdays, the wife's still fast asleep beside you snoring like a pig, you look out of the window and the sun's shining and you get that football-lucky feeling bubbling up inside you? "By Christ but," it says, "the lads are going to put some balls in the back of the net today."

Terence Not often of late.

Harry I haven't had it often myself recently, I must confess. But I got it this morning. That gentle nudge in my water. It said we won't put a foot wrong this afternoon.

Terence I hope you're right.

Harry Where's Randolph gone to for my glass of Scotch, I wonder? The Firth of bloody Forth? (*Another pause*) You know what my trouble is, of course? I hate bloody arguments. I can't stand rows. I'd walk barefoot from here to Wembley Stadium rather than face a barney. By rights, I shouldn't be the chairman of a football club, should I? (*Another pause*) You are right, of course. About him bringing the club into disrepute. And I will have to have it out with him about his love-life. Supposing we do win today, I'll really have a go at him, put things straight. Start next season off on an entirely different footing.

Terence What if we lose?

Harry Shall we face up to that particular bridge when we come to it?

Terence At the very most, it's only ninety minutes' football time away. If I were you, I'd start to think about it now. Win or lose, there are some who want him out.

Harry I still say he's a good manager.

Terence There are those that think otherwise.

Harry opens the window again and looks down into the ground. We can hear the crowd again, louder than before. Harry stands looking down for several moments

Randolph enters with the Scotch and soda

Harry closes the window

Harry Speak of the bloody devil, Randolph! I was just saying, did you have to go up to the distillery to get my drink?

Randolph There's a club called Distillery in Northern Ireland. Did you know? Distillery F.C.—Distillery Football Club. Trust the Irish, eh, to get drinking into sport. (*He hands Harry the glass*) Cheers. You did say you didn't want one, Mr Bullivant?

Terence No.

Randolph Only I'll tell you why it took so long, Mr Nicholls. With you saying tap discreetly on the door. I did knock quietly a couple of times and I don't think anybody heard me, so I had to hang about in the corridor like a spare part. Luckily, as things turned out, one of their directors came out of the board-room for a jimmy-riddle, so I tapped him up on his way back. Then Mr Gideon-Smith came out. Hey up, I managed to get a subscription from him for the wreath, even though we still don't know who it's for.

Harry Which one of their directors?

Randolph No, it was Mr Gideon-Smith who coughed up for the floral tribute—he gave me fifty p., in fact.

Harry I mean, which one of their directors went out to the bog?

Randolph I don't know his name—the big chap with the pot-belly and the laugh.

Harry Their chairman. Duggie Leadbetter. Did you tell him who the Scotch was for?

Randolph I might well have done.

Harry (*to Terence*) He's only disclosed my whereabouts to the very man I was trying to hide them from.

Randolph Why? Wasn't I supposed to say anything?

Harry (*with a long-suffering sigh*) Well done, Randolph—you've managed it again.

Randolph I'll tell you what: there are too many things to remember at this club. Something else that happened while I was waiting outside that board-room: their manager, Porter, sent his dogsbody round to lodge an official complaint. He collars me in the corridor.

Terence What about?

Randolph Nothing at all. It's all gamesmanship, isn't it? Doesn't it make you wild? It makes you wonder what they'll think of next to ruck about. He says to me, this dogsbody, "The loo's blocked up in the away team dressing-room." "What do you expect me to do about it?" I says "Unblock it," he has the cheek to say. I should cocoa. "If God had put me on this earth to unblock blocked-up loos," I said, "I'd have been born with a great long piece of wire in my hand."

Harry *Touché.*

Randolph Correct, Mr Nicholls. I gave him a mop and a bucket and a squeegee and told him to get on with it himself. "How are you off for bog paper in that loo?" I said. "All right, I think," he said. "Good," I said. "At least when it's unblocked you'll all be able to wipe your backsides," I said. "And that's more than our lads can do when we pay you a visit."

The door opens slightly and Douglas Leadbetter, the visiting club's chairman, peers into the office. He sees Harry and guffaws

Douglas So this is where you hide yourself away, is it, when you're on a losing run? Or am I interrupting something?

Harry Not at all, Douglas, old chap. Come in. Nice to see you after all these months. I just popped down here to have a word with our secretary.

Terence Good afternoon, Mr Leadbetter.

Douglas I hope you still think so when you've dropped two points at a quarter to five.

Harry Now—now. You'll have been in a game—it won't be all one-sided, believe you me.

Douglas I hope it isn't. Most sincerely. For the sake of the fans that we've brought down. What's gone wrong with your lot then, since the start of the season? You've really gone downhill, you have let it slide.

Harry You know what they say: it comes and it goes, in cycles.

Douglas Not at our place. (*Moving to the window*) We go from strength to strength. We power on—or I want to know the reason why. (*He peers down into the ground*)

Terence gives Harry a significant glance

Bugger me, what's happened to your gate? Don't they bother to come and watch you any longer? Not that you can blame them, eh?

Harry There's plenty of time—it's always a last-minute rush with our supporters.

Douglas It'll need to be. How many do you reckon there is down there now? Three thou?

Harry I'll bet there's nearer five. We're reckoning on some good support today. We need this one, you know, to save us going down.

Douglas No chance, Harry lad. We're taking both the points back with us, to clinch promotion. I should think most of those out there now are ours. We've got a special train-load of them down—so they're all ours, the ones with the railway-carriage light bulbs and the closet chains. And I'll bet we've passed two dozen coaches on the motorway, scarves hanging from the windows like Christmas decorations. We'll bump your gate up for you, never fear.

Harry (*coldly*) Many thanks.

Randolph delves into a cupboard

Douglas My pleasure—so long as your gatemen don't try to fiddle the turnstile receipts. My little joke. We've put the gates up everywhere we've played this season. They'll always pay to watch *good* football, won't they? Success breeds success. What do you say, Randolph?

Randolph surfaces with a bar of soap

Randolph What I say doesn't count much, does it? It's what the referee says that goes. And the word has been handed down, along the chain of echelon, via a linesman, that the referee's wash-basin is missing a cake of toilet soap. (*To Terence*) I bet that light-fingered dogsbody of theirs has stepped in and nicked it on their manager's say-so. I'll replenish the ref's dressing-room with this. (*He crosses to the door and pauses. His final remark, although addressed to Terence, is obviously intended for Douglas*) Even if we are propping up the table, there's nobody comes to this ground that has to cart along their own bum-paper and toilet soap. We might be struggling as a club, but we're still proud. *We* put shampoo in *both* our dressing-rooms.

Randolph goes out

Douglas (*sourly*) Every club has gone one—a joker, eh? Who is the referee, as a matter of interest?

Terence Liversedge. We've never had him before.

Douglas Liversedge? I've never even heard of him. Where does he hail from?

Terence Dartmouth.

Douglas Dartmouth? Bloody *Dartmouth*? That's in Devon, isn't it?

Terence It is unless they've moved it since yesterday.

Douglas Bloody hell-fire! They've swung one on you there, the Football League. His first-class rail fare from Devon to here doesn't bear thinking about. Plus his fee, plus his hotel bill, plus his dinner money last night. I'll tell you what, Harry, I don't care how big your crowd is this afternoon—Mr Liversedge will be going home with half your gate money in his pocket tonight.

Harry We always try to pay up with a smile—have you brought many guests with you today?

Douglas Only the usual gang of dedicated enthusiasts. We don't like to impose, but you can't keep them away, can you, when you're on a winning run?

Terence We wouldn't know.

Douglas If you'll excuse me, gentlemen, but I said I'd pop into our dressing-room before they go out. I did it by chance the day we thrashed the league leaders away from home—so the lads expect it from me every week now. Even when we're playing rubbish sides, present company excepted, of course. You know what superstitious footballers are like.

Douglas goes out

Harry I know what some club chairmen are like—piss-taking bastards.

Terence He's always been the same, that one.

Harry I hope he bloody chokes to death one day on one of his family-size pork pies. I'd love to see us win this afternoon, just this one time.

Terence I'd love to see us win every time.

Harry You know what they say, Terence—you can't win them all.

Terence No, but you can try. You can make some effort. You can win occasionally. We've won sod-all this season. And shall I tell you something? We'll win sod-all in the Fourth Division as well next season, unless there are some changes made.

Harry We're not down yet.

Terence We're as good as. We're only an hour-and-a-half's football from it.

Harry Not if we snatch it this afternoon.

Terence Some if.

Harry We've got to win today, haven't we? Or else . . .

Terence Or else what? That's the question.

Harry opens the window again and looks down. The crowd is chanting louder than ever

Harry Go on, lads, shout! I don't care how many coaches they brought down the motorway, or even if they had a couple of excursion trains— there are still more of ours than there are of theirs down there. Go on,

shout, you mad-headed buggers. Cheer. Cheer us on. See us through
this one, eh?

Gillian enters, returning with the work she took out with her

Gillian Have the teams come out on to the pitch?

Harry closes the window

Harry Not yet. But any moment now. Are you watching from up here or
in the stand?
Gillian Up here, I think.
Harry We could do with you outside, shouting, we need all the moral
support we can get.
Gillian Don't worry. I'll shout. You'll hear me through that window.
Harry Wish us through it if you can, as well.

Gillian holds up her hands to show that she has got her fingers crossed

Gillian And I said my prayers last night.
Terence Speaking of last night, Gillian, did you enjoy your meal?
Gillian What meal was that?
Terence Wasn't it a meal you had? Dinner or supper or whatever you
choose to call it?
Gillian Where? When?
Terence Didn't you go to the Royal for a sit-down spread?
Gillian No, Mr Bullivant. I haven't been into the Royal Hotel for over
a year, and then not into the restaurant.
Terence Do you know, it's funny, isn't it? I didn't think it could be you.
It was just something that somebody—this chap—happened to mention
this morning, in passing.
Gillian Oh, yes? What was that?
Terence Nothing worth mentioning. Although, actually, I'm pleased that
you've put things straight and cleared it up. I mean, I knew the fellow
must have got it partly wrong at least, because he said he'd thought he'd
seen you *and* Mr Gant.
Gillian If you're talking about the Royal Hotel last night, it certainly
wasn't me.
Terence I knew it couldn't have been Mr Gant.
Harry Bernie was away scouting last night, wasn't he? Didn't he go over
to the Rovers' ground to watch a seventeen-year-old of theirs in a
reserve team match?
Terence Well, I know, Mr Nicholls—that's just what I told this chap.
Gillian And as I wasn't in the Royal either, it seems he got us both wrong.
Terence So it would appear, Gillian.

*There is a sudden roar from the crowd, loud enough to be heard through the
closed window, as the teams run out on to the pitch*

Harry Is that them coming out now? (*He glances down out of the window*)

It is, you know. Go on, my lucky lads! I've been shirking my duties. I'd better get into that directors' box.

Bernie Gant enters from outside

Harry Have you got them going, then? Inspired them with eloquence? (*He displays a clenched fist*) Are they going to give it all they've got?
Bernie They're going to do their very best.
Terence Including Frankie Womersley?
Bernie Yes. Including Womersley.
Terence It'll surprise a few people, me included, if that young idle bugger pulls his finger out.
Harry You're not sitting on the bench today, then, Bernie?
Bernie I thought I'd give it a miss and come up into the box for this one. They're on their own out there anyway, I can't do it for them. I've tried to make them believe I'm confident. I wish I bloody was. But if I sit up in the box at least it looks as if I am. And if the team think so, a bit of it might rub off.

Another roar from the crowd outside which we hear, through the closed window. Harry glances down

Harry That's the opposition coming out.

Bernie also glances down through the window

Bernie He's a crafty bugger is their manager. He's heard my team-sheet and he's switched his positions. He's got O'Leary in the number two shirt.
Terence He's not allowed to change them.
Bernie He's bloody done it. That means he's shifted Denis Hennigan across to mark Womersley. It shows I'm not the only one that reckons Frankie as a possible match-winner.
Terence That has put the lid on it. He's a bloody animal is Hennigan. If he kicks Womersley early on, he won't want to see the ball again all afternoon.
Bernie Perhaps. On the other hand, if Hennigan does clog Frankie he might get him steamed up. Make him turn it on for us.
Harry Do you really think so?
Bernie I only said, he might.

Douglas Leadbetter enters from outside, on his way back from his visit to the away team dressing-room

Douglas I've done my duty—am I allowed to take the short cut back?
Harry Of course, Douglas, be my guest.
Douglas (*noticing Bernie and pretending surprise*) What is it, then, in here, a summit meeting or the gathering of the clans? The storm clouds darken, eh?

Harry We're all on our way to the directors' box. We were only waiting for you.

Douglas I'll bet you were planning tactical changes for the second half when you come out two nil down!

Harry gives him a cold, quick smile

Harry Ready, Terence?

Harry, Terence and Douglas move to the door. Bernie remains by the window

Bernie I'll be along before the kick-off—when the referee has come out.

Terence and Douglas go out

Harry pauses, holding up his hands with his fingers crossed

Harry Don't forget, Gillian.
Gillian (*copying his gesture*) I won't.
Harry The best of luck, then, Bernie.
Bernie The best of luck to all of us . . .

Harry goes out

We'll need it out there this afternoon.
Gillian You're going to need it more than just out there. The secretary's gunning for you.
Bernie How do you mean?
Gillian What I say. I mean the club secretary wants to shoot you dead. Bang-bang. He just took a practice shot at me.
Bernie When? (*He looks out of the window*)
Gillian Before you came in. He had a go for the chairman's benefit. He managed to drop it into the conversation that an anonymous friend of his had seen you and me together in the Royal Hotel last night.

Bernie's mind is on the game ahead, he is gazing out on the pitch and only giving half his attention to Gillian. It is some moments before her last sentence sinks in

Bernie We weren't in the Royal Hotel last night.
Gillian You don't have to tell me that. He was trying to mix it for us both—I presume you more than me.
Bernie The cheeky bugger. The crafty conniving sod. You put things straight, I trust?
Gillian I did my best.
Bernie Good girl.

Bernie turns his attention back to the football pitch

Holy Moses, will you look at that! We haven't even kicked off yet— they're still kicking in practice shots—and our keeper's already let two go through his legs. Mister Cement-boots himself. (*He turns back to Gillian*) Come here.

Gillian (*ignoring his final words*) The chairman stuck up for you though.

Bernie Good.

Gillian I thought you might like to know.

Bernie Thank God somebody does.

Gillian He said you were over at the Rovers' ground last night, watching a young reserve.

Bernie Yes, I had let that vague possibility drop—mostly as a smokescreen for the wife's benefit.

Gillian Oh.

Bernie You know me—I like to leave a few red herrings here and there—they can't do any harm. The Royal bloody Hotel, though, eh? Isn't it marvellous? We shoot off to some out-of-the-way God-forsaken country pub—I don't know how I'm going to claim the petrol money—we don't pass a soul we know, going or coming back. I was congratulating myself this morning on how we'd played a blinder last night. I was, while I was shaving: "Well done, Bernie son, ten out of ten." And now that cunning bugger cracks on we've been spotted somewhere we've never even stuck our noses in. You can't win really, can you? That's bloody life, is that. The Royal Hotel as well, no less! Is it likely we'd be out together in the Royal, you and me?

Gillian No. It isn't, is it?

Bernie We do try to play it careful, if nothing else.

Gillian Yes. We do.

Bernie Off we go. Here comes Jack-the-lad: the referee and his merry men. This is the big one, then. For Christ's sake, do it for me, my bonny lads. Let's have some bloody effort. It's all or nothing this afternoon. (*Back to Gillian*) I said "come here", you.

Gillian What for?

Bernie Give us a kiss for luck before the off.

Gillian If he does want shut of you, the secretary, you know he usually gets his way.

Bernie You said yourself, the chairman's on my side.

Gillian The chairman's been at the club two seasons. The secretary's been here longer than me. The secretary's run this club for donkey's years. If Terence Bullivant wants you out, Bernie, your days are numbered.

Bernie Why do you think I want this result so much this afternoon? If I keep them up, I'll be all right. I think. I have got some friends on the board. If we go down to the Fourth, I'm on my bike.

Gillian What happens then?

Bernie You've asked me that before today. I've already told you. The road to the Labour Exchange is littered with football managers of good intentions. I might get a stopgap job as a scout—an old pal's act from an old pal in the south. But that wouldn't even pay the rent. We've got to win today, that's all. And I don't think we can do it, but we've got to. If we lose I'm buggered up completely.

Gillian Pardon my selfishness, Bernie—I really meant what happens to me? To us? Am I on my bike as well as you?

Bernie Give it a break, girl, eh? Leave it till after the game.

Gillian No, Bernie. If this match means so much to you, aren't I entitled to know what it means to me? Am I on my bike again, Bernie, if we lose?

Bernie If I'm scratching an existence scouting in the south, and you're stuck up here—we wouldn't have a lot going for us, would we? It's muck or nettles this game for both of us, Gilly. We're not down yet though—fingers crossed, keep praying. I'm going down to the directors' box. Come on, give us a kiss and grope for luck before I go.

Gillian A kiss and a grope for luck. It isn't even sex, is it? It's football.

Bernie That can't be bad though, can it?

Gillian A kiss and a grope for luck. I should never have been born with boobs—I'd stand more chance with you if they were rabbit's feet.

He kisses her, and she allows his hand to move inside her clothing and feel her breasts

As they embrace, the door opens and Jacqueline Gant, Bernie's eighteen-year-old daughter, enters

Gillian and Bernie break apart, embarrassed

Bernie What the hell do you want, Jacqueline?

Jacqueline Two tickets for the game, Father.

Bernie They're on the gate.

Jacqueline shakes her head. Bernie turns to Gillian

Gillian I gave them to Randolph.

Bernie Jesus save us, the silly old sod forgot to leave them!

At which point, Randolph bustles in, flustered

Randolph They've delayed the kick-off. There's a right flap on out there. It's come to light at last who's kicked the bucket. You'll never guess—it'll come as a shock will this—it's the Vice-President of the Supporters' Club himself, Mr Raymond Harmsworth, as was. 'Course, it's flung us in a proper tizzy. There's two minutes' silence about to happen. By rights, all our players should have black arm-bands on. Now, where the hummers did I put them after we used them last time?

Gillian, Jacqueline and Bernie stand motionless as Randolph hunts through drawers and cupboards. From outside, over the loudspeakers, we hear the strains of "Abide With Me". Randolph stands to attention, awkwardly as—

the CURTAIN *falls*

ACT II

The same. An hour and three-quarters later

The game is in its closing seconds. Gillian is alone in the office and stands by the open window gazing down, motionless. We hear the roar of the spectators as the final whistle is blown—but Gillian does not move, and gives no indication as to which side has won. Moments later, we hear the pop music over the loudspeakers, playing the crowd out of the ground. Gillian closes the window but stays by it, looking down at the pitch. Harry Nicholls bursts excitedly into the office

Harry How about that, then? Three-bloody-nil! We ran rings round them, Gillian—they were never even in it! We slaughtered them.

Gillian smiles, but says nothing

Harry goes out, back the way he has come. Randolph enters, also excited

Randolph Marvellous, eh? Marvellous. What did I say before the game? In here? I said we were going to do it. That'll teach them—that might learn them a lesson. Perhaps they'll behave like professional footballers next season and equip themselves properly. Division Two? How can they think of themselves as Second Division contenders without loo-paper in their bog? They were two marvellous goals though, weren't they? Unstoppable. And Clayton took that penalty like a good 'un.

Harry returns, carrying a bottle of champagne

Harry Give this to Bernie, would you, Gillian, when he comes in, with my compliments. Tell him he'll be more than welcome to have one in the board-room too. Their chairman's face, you ought to see it—long as a mile. What about that, then, Randolph?

Randolph What about it, Mr Nicholls? What a marvellous result. You know what they say? "That's football." I can't get over it, I can't.

Harry Can't stop—I'm . . .

Harry jiggles a hand in the air to indicate drinking, and goes out

Randolph I shall be doing a bit of that myself in the Supporters' Club bar before the evening's very much older. There's only one sad thing about today's proceedings, Gillian. It's a great pity that the Vice-President of the Supporters' Club couldn't manage to hang on until a quarter to five this afternoon.

Gillian He had to answer a final whistle of his own, Randolph.

She has spoken ironically, but Randolph considers her words at their face value

Randolph True. True. Very astutely put. All the same, you'd have thought that whoever it is in charge up there might have granted the Vice-President a bit of injury time. Although, perhaps it's just as well. He'd have had a bloody heart attack watching that game today.

Terence bursts into the office, a Scotch and soda in his hand. Randolph turns to him

What about that, then, Mr Secretary?

Terence It's a great pity they couldn't have turned it on like that six months ago, instead of leaving it until today. We might really have had something to celebrate, like promotion to the Second instead of standing around patting ourselves on the back because we've managed to evade the drop.

Randolph Well, I never thought we would go down. I never saw us as Fourth Division material.

The telephone rings on Gillian's desk and she answers it

Gillian (*into the telephone*) City Ground. . . . Three nil, to us . . . That's right, three nil—it came as a surprise to us as well . . . Thank you. (*She replaces the phone*)

Harry returns yet again, carrying his own Scotch and soda, a vodka and tonic, a bottle of light ale and a glass

Harry Gillian, you are a vodka and tonic, I believe?

Gillian Thank you.

Harry Light ale for you, Randolph, that is your usual tipple?

Randolph Very much appreciated, Mr Chairman.

Harry I fail to see any reason why the celebrations should be entirely confined to the interior of the board-room. Besides, the atmosphere in here is more conducive—there's a few long faces in the board-room among the visiting directors and their guests.

Terence We haven't really done them any favours, condemning them to another season in the Third.

Harry Hey! It's only just occurred to me—another trip up there next season. One fish-paste sandwich and a sniff of the barmaid's apron, if we're lucky. They'll be even less hospitable next season after what we've done to them today.

Randolph It's going to be having to remember to put the toilet soap and the loo-paper on the coach that's bothering me.

The telephone rings. Gillian answers it

Gillian (*into the telephone*) City Ground. . . . Three nil, to us . . . That's right, three . . . Thank you, good afternoon. (*She puts down the phone*) That's the second one that couldn't believe his ears.

Harry I can't say I blame them. I found it difficult to believe my eyes sometimes, sitting out there this afternoon. Here's to us next season, anyway.

Terence Don't you think we ought to get this season over and done with first?

Harry It is, to all intents and purposes. We have to go through the motions for another week, but those two points this afternoon have put us out of danger. I'm optimistic for next season too. I think we saw the nucleus of a team this afternoon. They *played* like a football team: they ran for each other; they helped each other out; they looked for spaces. And what about those two goals of Womersley's?

Randolph Oh, didn't he take them well, Mr Chairman? Especially the second?

Harry Exceptionally well. Next season then—cheers.

Randolph Next season—and very many of 'em—goals.

They all drink. With them, we become aware of a sound coming from the ground

Harry What's that?

Harry crosses to the window and opens it. We can hear the voices of supporters as they chant out the manager's name: "Ber—nie Gant, Ber—nie Gant, Ber—nie Gant", etc. Harry glances down

They're shouting for the manager. There's about fifty of them, supporters, outside the front office. (*He shuts the window*)

Randolph He's not come up yet, Mr Chairman, from the dressing-room.

Terence You'd think he'd won a gallon of whisky for the Manager of the Month award. And if we'd lost today they'd have been stood in just the same place, screaming for his guts for corner-flags.

Randolph You know what they say, Mr Secretary: "That's football."

Terence gives Randolph a baleful glance, puts down his empty glass and moves to leave

Douglas Leadbetter enters from the board-room, and Terence passes him

Harry Hard cheese, Douglas. Better luck next season, eh?

Douglas I'm not surprised to find you all skulking in here again. You must be thoroughly ashamed of what went on out there this afternoon under the guise of football.

Harry Weren't you satisfied with the result, then, Douglas?

Douglas I wasn't satisfied with the manner in which the game was played. Or with the standard of refereeing, either. Mr Liversedge, of Dartmouth, will be travelling back to Devon in the knowledge that there'll be a card submitted to the Football League giving him one mark out of ten from me.

Harry How very odd. I've got him marked down for a nine on my card.

Douglas You must be joking. He never left the centre-circle. He allowed your players to get away with murder. That number five of yours, the big, ugly bugger, was kicking lumps off of little Anderson for ninety minutes non-stop. Our right full-back executes a perfectly fair and legitimate tackle a good two yards outside the area—and he gives a penalty against him.

Harry It looked a good penalty from where I was sitting.

Douglas It looked a good dive. Your front runner deserves a medal from the Amateur Swimming Board.

Harry Your right full-back went in from behind.

Douglas And your number ten performed an impeccable double-reverse somersault and jack-knife. With pike. (*He holds up two imaginary number-boards in the manner of a swimming judge*) Nine-and-a-half, nine-and-a-half, nine-and-a-half, ten.

Harry (*with a wink at Randolph*) You know what they say, Douglas: "That's football."

At which point, Bernie enters, having come from the dressing-rooms

Congratulations, Bernie—well done. Are the lads all right?

Bernie Apart from one or two knocks and stud-marks. That Hennigan of theirs is a monster, isn't he? He ought to be in Hammer films with bolts through his neck and big thick boots on. Hello, Mr Leadbetter, hard luck—I didn't see you standing there.

Douglas Congratulations, Mr Gant. I won't say you deserved it, because I didn't think you did. (*Back to Harry*) I assume it is all right for me to use your stairs again?

Harry Naturally, Douglas. What else are friends for?

Douglas moves to leave, then pauses

Douglas I always go down and have a word with our lads in the bath—always—win or lose, after every match. Some of us still try to maintain some of the old-fashioned standards, in a world of fast-diminishing sporting values.

Douglas goes out

Bernie makes a two-fingered gesture after Douglas

Bernie And that goes for his manky black puddings as well.

Randolph I almost asked him for a donation to the Supporters' Club's Vice-President's floral tribute—only I thought it might be adding insult to injury.

Harry (*to Bernie*) Well done again. They played a blinder, all of them.

Bernie We got the breaks for once, that made a change.

Harry You were right about playing Womersley.

Bernie I was right about Hennigan striping him. There was no holding Frankie after that dirty animal kicked him up the arse.

Randolph Well, I think they justified themselves out on that park today them lads, Mr Chairman. There's no other word for it, they justified themselves. They turned into men from boys. They rose to the occasion.

Harry They did well.

Randolph Do you want to know what I think? And I've been giving it some thought. I think they managed to find that little extra as a mark of respect for the late, deceased Vice-President. They went out there with their heads held high and did it in his memory. Bloody hell-fire! I know what I have forgotten to do. Get them black arm-bands back from the dressing-room. If I know those young players, they'll take them off and sling them down with the mucky kit, and they'll get covered in mud and blood and stink to high heaven of liniment. Else worse still, they'll chuck them in the bath and block the drains up.

Randolph goes out

Harry There was a crowd of supporters outside the front office five minutes since, shouting for you.

Bernie They'll either wait or bugger off.

Harry You should pop down and give them a wave at least—they are the ones that pay the money at the gate.

Bernie Right-ho.

Harry And I ought to be doing my duty as well, instead of standing here. I ought to be in the board-room playing host. Are you coming down?

Bernie In a minute. There's one or two bits of administration I want to do before I go tonight—we've got a game on Monday.

Harry A reserve team fixture. It can wait till Monday morning, surely?

Bernie The next game's always more important than the last. Besides, you know what a forgetful bugger Randolph is. If we leave it to him there'll be no coach booked or kit arranged. We'll have to walk up there and play the match in Y-fronts, shoes and socks and bloody black arm-bands.

Gillian The coach is booked. Two o'clock here at the ground. And we're playing in the all-white strip which is back from the laundress first thing Monday morning.

Bernie Good lass.

Harry You've no excuse, then. Go and show yourself to the fans and then come and have a celebratory one or two with me and the directors.

Bernie In a minute.

Harry moves to the door. He knows that Bernie is staying behind to chat up Gillian, and he feels that he ought to say something but cannot bring himself to do so

Harry Bernie . . . ?

Bernie Yes?

Harry There's a bottle of champagne over there. I brought it in for you in a sudden burst of wild enthusiasm as soon as the whistle went.

Bernie Many thanks, Harry.

Harry My pleasure. Anyway, it's there. If you feel like taking it home tonight and watching Match of the Day with the missis with a bit of style and elegance.

Bernie Something like that, I suppose. Cheers.

Harry I'll see you shortly in the board-room.

Harry goes out

Bernie picks up the bottle of champagne, examines it, and puts it down again

Bernie He's a likeable chap, our chairman, but underneath that amiable surface lies a spineless bugger.

Gillian He always speaks well of you.

Bernie I know. I'm beginning to wish he didn't. Well?

Gillian Well what?

Bernie Well, haven't you got anything to say?

Gillian Well done. Congratulations.

Bernie Stop at "well done". Don't *you* start congratulating me. I've done nothing out there. I'm as surprised as anybody. I wouldn't have backed that side today with washers—and then they go out and set the park alight. I don't know. You spend all day and every day right through the season trying to get them to play it your way: telling them, teaching them, showing them, demonstrating, begging, pleading, threatening, explaining—sometimes in training they even get it right, not often, but enough to make you think you just begin to see that little glimmer of light. And then match day comes and they trot out on the pitch and let you down as regular as clockwork. They've either got it, footballers, or they haven't—and if it isn't inside them at the off then not all the coaching in the world can put it there. I'd decided this lot hadn't got it. I had, I'd given up. And then this afternoon they slot it together and the sun shines down. It did. What was I saying earlier? Did you notice how the sun came out at kick-off time? Don't try to tell me there isn't somebody up there that doesn't like the game.

Gillian Perhaps Randolph's theory's right—perhaps they did turn it on in memory of the deceased Vice-President.

Bernie (*picking up the bottle of champagne again*) Bloody champagne yet. And if we'd have lost they'd have had you stamping up my cards by now.

Gillian That, as Randolph would say, is football.

Bernie It seems we're both still on the retained list for next season. I'm down on the club's team sheet and you're name's back on mine. Why don't you take this bottle round to your place and bung it in the fridge. I'll be round as soon as I've shown my face where needed, made my excuses and done the necessaries with the wife.

Gillian You mean you'll come round then and "do the necessaries" with me? What was it the chairman said? A bit of style and elegance with Match of the Day? No, thanks, Bernie. I don't think we've got a fixture going tonight.

He looks at her, puzzled, and she holds his glance

Randolph enters with a handful of bedraggled black arm-bands

Randolph I *was* too late. Just look at the state of these! There's two gone missing altogether and three of these have come apart at the seams.

And look at this one here. (*He holds up an arm-band that has been stretched beyond recognition*) You won't believe what I'm going to tell you now, but Tosher Armitage was sitting in the bath, as large as life, with this stretched round his head. He was pretending to be an Apache warrior—playing at Geronimos. Bloody footballers! I'm not kidding, if that's how adult men are supposed to behave in the prime of life, I'm only grateful I'm a senior citizen.

Gillian We'll have to buy some new ones, Randolph.

Randolph You can't *get* new ones, that's just my point. You tell me where you can buy black arm-bands in these enlightened times? They don't go in for bereavement any longer—not on a long-term policy. I've got to dash down now to the players' bar. The substitute's supposed to be in there with his one in his trouser pocket. (*He goes to the door and pauses*) I'll tell you this much, though, we'll have to do something about getting some replacements from somewhere. It shan't be long before we're wanting them again—The Supporters' Club Treasurer hasn't ventured far this season—he's knocking on for eighty-three.

Randolph goes out

Bernie Talk about priorities—we do the impossible, the Houdini act, we snatch both points—and there's that cantankerous, forgetful old devil doing his pieces about a couple of black, bloody arm-bands.

Gillian Trust Randolph.

Bernie On the subject of priorities—how are we fixed then, for later on tonight?

Gillian I'm going to leave it out.

Bernie What's upset you? Because our Jacqueline walked in?

Gillian It's got nothing to do with Jacqueline.

Bernie Why then? Come on—we won. That's all I care about. Don't you care, madam, that you can put your bike away?

The telephone rings. Gillian answers it

Gillian (*into the telephone*) City ground. . . . Hang on a second. (*She puts her hand over the mouthpiece and says to Bernie*) It's one of the newspapers wanting details.

Bernie I've got to go down and smile at the fans, then drop in and watch the chairman and the board gloat and swagger in the board-room. I'll see you soon.

Bernie goes out

Gillian (*into the telephone*) Hello? . . . It was, yes, three nil to us . . . Very good indeed . . . (*She refers to a notebook*) Frankie Womersley in the twenty-seventh minute . . . Womersley—W—O—M—E—R—S—L—E—Y—Frankie—I—E . . . Yes, a couple of seasons ago in the under eighteen's . . . A penalty in the fifty-third minute, taken by Dickie Clayton . . . Then the third one in the eighty-fifth, again by Womersley . . . Thank you very much, good-bye.

Gillian puts down the phone. She goes and picks up the champagne bottle, studies it, then puts it down again. There is a knock on the door

Yes?

Jacqueline Gant enters

Jacqueline I'm looking for my father—is he about?

Gillian He was a moment ago, Jacqueline. He's dodging around at the moment, all over the place, I don't know where you'd find him. He did say he'd be coming back here though. Would you like to wait?

Jacqueline Yes. All right. I will.

Gillian Sit down.

Jacqueline Thanks.

Jacqueline sits. Gillian bustles about the office, but putting on a show of being more busy than she really is

Gillian Did you enjoy the match?

Jacqueline Yes, thanks. He got his result. Look, I won't wait. My mother's sitting at a table by herself in the Supporters' Club bar. Perhaps you'd give him a message—I might as well tell you as him.

Gillian Yes—of course I will.

Jacqueline When I came in here for the tickets—earlier on—and caught him slobbering over you—would you just tell him that I haven't said anything, to my mother.

Gillian Yes, I will. But it wasn't exactly slobbering.

Jacqueline You had me fooled then—it was a very good imitation.

Gillian I'll tell your father what you said, Jacqueline—thank you, anyway.

Jacqueline Don't you thank me, and he needn't either if it comes to that— I'm keeping what I saw to myself for her sake, not yours or his.

Gillian I understand that.

Jacqueline Do you? I shouldn't think you understood much about my parents' marriage, or cared much, either.

Gillian Frankly, Jacqueline, not a bloody sausage—and that's swearing. And if you'd like proof of that I'm perfectly willing to walk down into the Supporters' Club, now, and tell your mother, to her face, that I've had something going with her husband now for over eighteen months. Well? Would you like me to do that?

Jacqueline I should think that's the last thing in the world you'd do.

Gillian Try me. Dare me.

Jacqueline Why should I? Why should *you*?

Gillian Supposing I wanted him to leave her and come and live with me?

Jacqueline That's something he'd never do in a million years.

Gillian Are you sure of that?

Jacqueline Positive.

Gillian Jacqueline, a week last Wednesday night there was a knock on my door. Your father was standing outside with his holdall in his hand. "I've done it, Gillian," he said. "I've left the wife."

Jacqueline That isn't true.

Gillian You were at college—you wouldn't know.

Jacqueline I'd have been told.

Gillian But you weren't. Would you like to hear? He moved in with me on the Wednesday and on the following night he went to a reserve team game. He came back to the flat at four o'clock in the morning. He'd palled up with a friend of his and they'd been to a drinking club and they'd stood there, at the bar, after time, talking football. I was blazing mad. He was stone cold sober, too. That made it worse. If he'd come back blue-blind paralytic I could have understood it—but to stay out until four o'clock, just talking football, on the second night after he'd moved in with me . . . Then, funnily enough, in another way, I was quite pleased. You see, I'd been going about with him for eighteen months and we'd never had a proper row. I'd been scared of rows while he'd been living with Joyce. I mean, if he'd fallen out with me, and not made it up, and then gone home to her—was a terrible thought. But when he walked in at four that morning, I thought, "Right, you awkward bugger, you're mine now, you belong to me, I can say what I like, I can do what I like". And I really let him have it because I suppose it had been building up for a year and a half. I threw a coat-hanger at him. Not one of the wire contraptions, one of the wooden, heavy, old-fashioned sort. But it didn't turn into a row. He didn't shout back, he just stood there, quiet. "Thanks very much," he said. "That's all I need. I can go back to the other one if I want coat-hangers slung at me." And he did. He went back to your mother that same day. Do you know what I found out afterwards? He hadn't even told your mother when he came to me that he was leaving her. He'd told her he was going up to Scotland for a few days to sign a player. He was leaving himself covered both ways—in case it didn't work out.

The telephone rings. Gillian picks it up

(*To Jacqueline*) Will you excuse me a moment? (*Into the telephone*) Hello, City ground. . . . They did, yes, three nil . . . Yes, it was a good result . . . So do I—I hope things start to pick up all round. (*She puts the telephone down*) So where was I? Oh yes, apropos me and your father. I just wanted you to know that it *was* more than a quick snog in this office, Jacqueline—it went as far as him coming to live with me for two whole days. Chalk that one up as another thing your mother didn't hear about. That was what hurt my pride the most—he came to live with me and it wasn't even important enough for him to tell his wife about.

Jacqueline He's always been the same, my father. He doesn't think, you know. No, that's not true—he *does* think. He thinks football twenty-four hours a day. And everything else—*anything* else takes second place. What most of us consider the important things in life, like human relationships—having responsibilities towards other people—to him that's incidental, life to him is background material for what happens on a football pitch between three o'clock and a quarter to five on a Saturday afternoon. You say your pride's been hurt. My mother's

social life, for years and years and years has been spent in waiting for
my father, just as I know she's waiting now, clutching her handbag,
twiddling with her gloves, sitting in miserable supporters' clubs, tatty
players' bars, moth-eaten ladies' rooms, in dreary football grounds all
over England. Don't you talk about losing pride.

Gillian You're right. I haven't got any pride. Even after he went back
home, I've settled for drifting back to the way things were before. Meeting
him at peculiar hours in peculiar drinking clubs, charging miles to spend
the odd half-hour with him in some back-street pub on the other side of
town. Having this unspoken arrangement again that we only go back to
my flat after it's dark. If you knew how many fly-bitten Chinese res-
taurants I've eaten in because there's nobody goes in there we know—
and I'm not even mad about Chinese food. Carrying on in lay-bys in the
back of a car. Never settle for the back of a car, Jacqueline. It's not very
very pleasant, it's not very comfortable and it's not very dignified. And
that just about sums up my life-style over the past year and a half:
unpleasant, uncomfortable, undignified. Thank God it's over. I must
have been out of my mind.

Jacqueline It didn't look as if it was over before the kick-off this afternoon.

Gillian No. But it was when the final whistle was blown. I was told, before
the match, if we lost—if he got the sack—that I'd be back in the saddle
of my bike. I've been climbing on to that bicycle so many times these
past few months, I'm getting saddle-sores. When the game was over,
and we'd won, I knew that meant another season for him here—and I'd
have another season of him being there. Perhaps the next time he left
home, he might remember to leave his front door key behind. I was
standing by that window, and I watched the team run off the park.
You'd have thought I would have felt relief. I didn't, though. Just a
bit empty inside. I knew I couldn't *stand* another season. To use one of
your father's expressions, Jacqueline—it isn't worth the effing aggro.
Besides, who wants to spend their life being a bad second to football?

Jacqueline Only my mother, I suppose—but then, she hasn't got much
choice.

*Terence enters, pauses, looking from Gillian to Jacqueline, sensing an
atmosphere*

Terence (*eventually*) Hello, Jacqueline—did you enjoy the game?

Jacqueline Not a lot, no. But at least the result was right.

Terence It did for me. As a matter of fact. I'm looking for your father—
any ideas?

Jacqueline No, I'm just about to give up waiting for him.

Gillian He could be in the board-room.

Terence I've just come from there myself.

Gillian In which case, I haven't a clue. He set off to see the fans, outside
the ticket office, but he must have moved on since then.

Terence They seek him here, they seek him there . . .

Randolph enters and holds up a solitary black arm-band

Randolph The last of the Mohicans—this is it. One black arm-band bereaving footballers for the use of, retrieved more by good luck than management from the substitute in the players' bar. Nudger Olliphant. He was trying to tell the barman it was a stripper's garter. He was—he was kidding on he'd been to a stag-night last Thursday and one of the strippers had given him her garter for favours received. It's only the club's official funereal insignia, and there's me laddo there, Olliphant, as large as life, trying to swop it with the barman for a light ale! I tell you—footballers, I've shot 'em!

Terence I don't suppose you happened to notice if Mr Gant was in the players' bar?

Randolph He isn't, no. Well he wasn't, to my certain knowledge—I took particular note of the fact as I came out.

Terence You didn't happen to take particular note of where he *is*, by any remote chance?

Randolph I'm afraid not, Mr Bullivant. But I can tell you somewhere else he wasn't, though. He wasn't in the Supporters' Club either. Your mother's in there, Jacqueline, sitting in the corner by the one-armed bandit.

Jacqueline Is she on her own?

Randolph To all intents and purposes. That elderly chap with the bald head under a trilby hat was having a word with her—(*to Gillian*)—the one we thought had popped his clogs in earlier on before we realized that it was Mr Raymond Harmsworth that had had the great misfortune to cross over to the other side on this day of all days. (*Back to Jacqueline*) I think he was asking her if she had change for a fifty pence piece while he was waiting for the fruit machine to become available: that's the fellow with the trilby hat, not the Vice-President deceased. Apart from that she was on her own.

Jacqueline I suppose I'd better get down there then.

Jacqueline moves towards the door

Randolph (*detaining her*) Jacqueline . . .

Jacqueline pauses

Don't waste your money on the one-armed bandit, will you? The jackpot went at three minutes to five this afternoon.

Jacqueline (*drily*) Thanks for the tip.

Jacqueline goes out

Randolph continues his anecdote to Gillian and Terence

Randolph There must have been well over a fiver in it, because it hadn't been emptied since the Supporters' Club Fund-Raising Mashed Pea and Pie Dance, and that was two Saturdays since. 'Course, I don't need to tell you who had it out this afternoon, do I?

Gillian Who was that?

Randolph One of their supporters, naturally. He had a big red and white rosette in his buttonhole, so he couldn't have been one of ours, could he?

Gillian Not unless we changed our colours as soon as the referee blew full-time.

Randolph Precisely. It's damn well infuriating, isn't it? There's our loyal supporters have fed that fruit machine, sparing no expense, for a fortnight, and then one of their ignorant hooligans walks in, sticks one five-pence piece in the slot—that's all, just one, it was his first—and cops on for the ruddy lot.

Terence You can't expect to win them all, Randolph.

Randolph No, but you know what they say about he who laughs last? You'll appreciate this. He was standing there, this fan of theirs—this Herbert—with his fists full of five-pence pieces, so I shouts across at him: "If I was you I'd make the most of that," I says. "Because it's all you will win this season—you can't get promotion out of one-armed bandits," I said.

Terence I'll bet that amused him.

Randolph Not really. "Piss off"', he shouted back, you'll pardon my swearing, Gillian. But they've always been the same, that lot: loud-mouthed, crude, and no sense of humour.

Terence That's one of the funny things about football—nobody else's supporters are ever as well-mannered and fair-minded as your own.

Randolph I'll say one thing for him though. He did make a donation in respect of the Vice-President's wreath.

Gillian You can't really ask for more than that, Randolph.

Randolph I said to him, "Would you care to contribute ten p. towards a floral tribute, we're burying our Vice-President." "Certainly," he said. "Here's twenty p.—bury your whole buggering team at the same time."

At which point, Harry Nicholls enters from the board-room. He is carrying another bottle of champagne, already opened, and a couple of glasses

Harry (*holding up the bottle*) Another little Indian. Champagne corks are popping in that board-room like bonfire night. Compliments of the chairman to the office staff, and will they join him in a celebratory one? (*He offers Gillian a glass*) Gillian?

Gillian (*taking it*) Thank you.

Harry Have you got any odd glasses knocking about the office anywhere, Randolph?

Randolph None that are opportune to the occasion, Mister Chairman. No champagne glasses.

Harry It doesn't matter what kind—any sort will do.

Randolph locates some cups and glasses, of various shapes and sizes, in a cupboard. Harry proffers the other champagne glass to Terence

Will you take a glass in here with me, Terence?

Terence Thanks.

Randolph (*displaying his array of cups and glasses*) Will these suffice?

Harry Those look entirely opportune to me, Randolph. (*He pours out champagne*) I'm not sure I should be offering you a drink in here, Terry. By rights, you should be doing the honours in the board-room. Entertaining guests. I didn't see you leave. I wondered where you'd disappeared to.

Terence I had a bit of business on.

Bernie Gant enters from outside. He is wearing a cardboard top-hat painted black and amber, and he is holding a plastic beaker

Harry Here comes the man of the moment. You're just in time, Bernie.

Bernie More champagne? You'd think we'd won the European Cup.

Harry We will, given time—if we continue to play like we did this afternoon. Celebrate when you can, that's my motto. It doesn't often happen in this game. There are more bad times than good.

Bernie (*taking a glass*) Does it go with Scotch? I got waylaid by the local press-man outside our dressing-room, while he was rabbiting on, spouting a load of rubbish, one of the supporters stuck a double whisky in my hand and this on my nut. (*He gets rid of the top-hat and the beaker*)

Gillian Did you see your Jacqueline on your way up?

Bernie No? Should I have done?

Gillian She was up here, looking for you.

Bernie Was it anything important, did she say, or something that could wait?

Gillian It was something she wanted to tell you—she seemed to think it was important.

Randolph If you want to find her, Mr Gant, I think you'll find she's gone down to the Supporters' Club to keep Mrs Gant company.

Bernie Whatever it is, I expect it'll keep until I can get down there myself. (*To Harry*) Frankie Womersley nobbled me in the corridor outside the dressing-room, I've had him on my back again.

Harry What about?

Bernie About a transfer. I told him before the kick-off, if he turned it on for me this afternoon, I'd think about it, I'd give it every consideration.

Terence And what have you just told him now?

Bernie I told him I've given it every consideration and thought about it— he can't have one.

Harry I bet that didn't exactly send him over the moon.

Bernie I'll handle Frankie Womersley. He's the least of my problems at this particular moment—I've just had to give the feller from the local rag a real right bollocking.

Harry Why was that?

Bernie We coast home three nil, and he has the gall to ask me if I thought our penalty was a dive, whether the first goal was offside, and had the ball gone over the dead-ball line before Stevens got his cross over and Womersley knocked the third one in? And they call themselves football reporters! I thought the local press was supposed to be on *our* side?

Terence Whatever gave you that idea? Who was it in the press-box today? Was if Cliff Braithwaite, or the young lad they send sometimes instead of him?

Bernie The young lad, naturally. He got a right mouthful from me, I tell you.

The door to the stairs opens cautiously, and Douglas Leadbetter peers in, on his way back from the dressing-room

Douglas Just passing through again—am I all right?

Harry Come in, Douglas, why not? We're only discussing club business. Honest to God, you'd think our general office was King's Cross Station the way you chuff through it! Will you take a drink with me as well?

Douglas Go on. I've got to face you twice next year again, so I won't part enemies today. Champagne is that? For missing relegation? Bugger me! We only brought three dozen bottles of light ale with us—and that was for celebrating if we got promotion! By bloody hell, it must be wonderful to be unsuccessful.

Harry Watch us next year, and then say that, Mr Chairman. (*He raises his glass*) Here's to us next season, then—in the League and competition.

Douglas I'll drink with you, Mr Chairman, but I'll not drink *to* you. I shall drink to my own lads. Here's to them. And may they be blessed with better refereeing than they've had today.

Randolph, slightly carried away with the sense of occasion, adds his own toast

Randolph Coupled with the name of the past Vice-President of the Supporters' Club deceased, Mr Raymond Harmsworth.

Harry, Terence and Douglas glower at Randolph. Bernie looks across the office at Gillian

Bernie Cheers, then.

Gillian Cheers.

They all drink, with the exception of Randolph, who only pretends to. Douglas, having downed his champagne, thumps at his chest, and grimaces

Douglas Jumping Jesus! There's some acid in that! I shall suffer for that little indiscretion on the coach drive back. Champagne plays up holy hell with my tummy—unless it's a vintage bubbly, of course. That's the trouble with playing away from home. It's not the quantity you drink—it's the quality of what you're offered.

Harry (*pointedly*) There are some clubs we've been to, where we'd have been grateful for a half of bitter and a packet of smoky bacon crisps.

But Douglas fails to grasp the implication

Douglas I've got a very good idea which club you mean as well. We were there ourselves the week before last. There are some stingy sods in the Third Division. Right then, Mr Chairman, are you offering me the hospitality of your board-room? Or shall I go away and talk behind *your* back?

Harry Come on, Mr Chairman, I'll open a bottle of Scotch for you alone.

Bernie watches Randolph curiously from time to time during the following. Harry holds the door open for Douglas, who pauses before going out

Douglas And let's see if your board-room pork pie is any better than it was last season—or is it still the same one?

With which, Douglas goes out

Harry shakes his head disbelievingly

Harry You can't win, can you? Come on, Terence, stand by me, lad. It's going to be a long, hard evening—it's got all the portents. You've got broad shoulders. See me through it. Bernie, are you going to grace the board-room with your presence?

Terence goes to the door

Bernie I'll be along in a minute.
Terence You won't shoot off anywhere? I do still want a word with you.
Bernie I'm coming down to the board-room—very shortly.
Terence I meant in private.

Terence follows Harry out

Bernie What's the matter, Randolph? You've been fiddling and faffing around with that glass. Don't you like champagne?
Gillian Pass it to me if you don't fancy it, Randolph.
Randolph It isn't that. It comes as no great innovation to me, champagne. I've got a bottle of the stuff at home that I won in the Tombola at the Supporters' Club Dinner and Dance. It's still unopened on the sideboard.
Bernie He's one of the bloody jet-set, is Randolph, champagne on the sideboard.
Randolph Only I thought I'd whip this one down to Enid—you know, Mrs Howson behind the counter in the season ticket-holders' tea-room. She's a bit upset about the passing of the late lamented Vice-President—he's had one without sugar from her, and an eccles cake every home game for donkey's seasons.
Bernie There's no bloody eccles cakes where he's gone to. Go on, you'd better get off, Randolph, before it goes flat.
Randolph I shan't be long.
Bernie Hey! And if you happen to glance inside the Supporters' Club, you might shout across and tell my good lady I shall be tied up for a while with the chairman and co in the board-room.
Randolph I'll make a specific point of popping in.

Randolph goes out

A pause. Bernie opens the window and glances down

Bernie There's not much to show, looking down there, is there, for nine months' toil and hard slog? A ground full of litter and the turf worn off the pitch. Stud-marks, beer-bottles, old programmes, fag-ends, and a few broken hearts. Bring on the groundsman and the sweeper-up.

Gillian You kept them in the Third Division, there's that.

Bernie That was no achievement—that was a face-saving act. I nearly took the buggers down, which is more to the point.

Gillian Look towards next season for achievement.

Bernie Have you had second thoughts since I spoke to you last?

Gillian About what?

Bernie About tonight What's happening?

Gillian Nothing, Bernie. Nothing's happening tonight. Not as far as we're concerned. No, I haven't had second thoughts.

Bernie Think about it now, then. The wife won't hang about. She'll have a drink downstairs and then get on her bike. She won't expect to see me now, not now we've won.

Gillian No—she won't, will she?

Bernie I shall have to put my nose inside the board-room, naturally.

Gillian Naturally.

Bernie If only for the sake of appearances. Have a couple in there at least. But I could duck away and meet you again about seven o'clock—seven-thirty.

Gillian No, thanks.

Bernie Why not?

Gillian Has it ever struck you, Bernie, that there's been one lady's bike too many parked outside this club for far too long?

Bernie Christ Almighty, Gillian, you're not going to start on the jealousy bit? Not tonight? That game today has knackered me out, physically and mentally. I'm in no mood this evening for bitter argument.

Gillian No, Bernie—never again.

Bernie So let's meet up later on somewhere for a quiet, civilized drink.

Gillian Sorry.

Bernie Why bloody not?

Gillian Because I don't want to, Bernie.

Bernie Well, what the maring hell *do* you want?

Gillian In football parlance, Bernie, in words you understand, shall I tell you? A free transfer, that's all—I want away from you.

Bernie You can have one of them, madam, if that's what you want!

Gillian Not from you—because you can't give me one, I'm not under contract to you, Bernie, I never was. I can negotiate my own terms, wherever I choose.

Bernie What's brought this on all of a sudden?

Gillian It isn't all of a sudden . . .

Bernie It is to me . . .

Gillian Not to me it isn't. I've had enough, Bernie, it's as simple as that. I've had it up to here with football.

Bernie It's the end of the season, we're all choked to death with football.

Gillian I don't *mean* that. I mean I'm fed up with having football run my life—like after a match, when how many hours I get with you depends on whether you've won or lost. Like *before* a match. I mean, putting it at its lowest level, I prefer to think of my tits as symbols of my female sexuality, or even just as mammary glands—they are not, and never have been, no more than a pair of lucky mascots.

Bernie You're not still going on about that? About Jacqueline walking in?

Gillian It's got nothing to do with Jacqueline.

Bernie Yes, it has. You said that she came back? What for? What did she say when she came back up here?

Gillian Nothing. As a matter of fact, she came back to tell you that you needn't worry—that she hadn't told Joyce about catching us at it. She needn't have bothered really, should she? It never even crossed your mind that she would say anything, did it?

Bernie Yes, of course it did. But at the time, if you'll cast your mind back, I did have other things to think about.

Gillian Of course, the match.

Bernie Yes, is anything wrong with that?

Gillian No, football first, as always.

Bernie Yes, football first, why not? It's all sweat and slog to survive at all in this game and I have to survive, it's my living.

Gillian Well, you survived today. And that was what was most important. And they're waiting for you now, inside the board-room. The chairman, the board of directors, glasses raised, champagne bottles at the ready. They want to tell you what a wonderful chap you are. You'd better get in there, Bernie.

Bernie I told you before, I've got to show my face.

Gillian For the sake of appearances.

Bernie A couple of drinks, that's all, and I'll duck straight out again. Meet me somewhere.

Gillian Sorry, Bernie. It's been a long, hard afternoon for me as well. I'm going home this evening.

Bernie Take that bottle of champagne with you then. Stick it in the fridge. As soon as I can get away I'll come round to your place.

Gillian Would that be after it was dark, Bernie, or would it be in the hours of daylight?

Bernie Wait here for me. Twenty minutes at the most. I'll come home with you.

They hold each other's gaze for several moments, then Gillian slowly shakes her head

If you do go, Gill, the champagne's there, for both of us, if you want to take it.

Bernie goes out

Gillian picks up the bottle of champagne, smiles sadly, and puts it down again as the phone rings. She picks up the phone

Gillian City ground, hello? . . . Yes, they did, three nil . . . Yes, they will, they'll be in the Third Division again next season . . . Good afternoon. (*She puts the phone down*)

There is a knock on the outside door

Yes? Come in.

Frankie Womersley enters, spruced up, his hair still damp from the bath

Yes?

Frankie Is he up this end anywhere?

Gillian Is who up this end anywhere?

Frankie The big boss—your friend—Gantie.

Gillian I'm afraid you've just this minute missed him. He's gone into the board-room.

Frankie Boozing it up, is he? Putting a few down to celebrate the two goals I knocked in for him? Is that through there, is it?

Gillian Whatever you want with Bernie Gant, if you walk through that door you'll be going the wrong way about getting it.

Frankie I want a move, don't I, darling? I want away from this Mickey Mouse Football Club.

Gillian If you want to talk about a transfer, Frankie, take my word and pick another moment—he isn't in the right mood. I thought you'd already had a word with him?

Frankie Two words. Third time lucky, maybe. He's turned me down twice today, the evil bastard.

Gillian I should think he's doing what he thinks best for the club.

Frankie Oh, undoubtedly. And I'll do what I think best for Frankie Womersley. Sod Gantie. I'll go to the top dog instead. Ooojamaflip— the chairman—what-he-call-himself? Nicholls, is it? Is he in there as well, is he?

Gillian If the manager's told you "no", there's not much point in seeing the chairman. But if you want to wait around for anything up to a couple of hours, do so.

Frankie A couple of hours?

Gillian They escaped the drop today, remember?

Frankie (*after considering*) Fair enough. I can't hang about, I've got something lined up in the Supporters' Club.

Gillian That'll make a nice change for you. Which one is it tonight? The one that props up the juke-box, with her eyelashes down to her knees and her skirt up to her bum, or that little blonde—the one that models?

Frankie Which one that models?

Gillian The one that models flat on her back underneath the season ticket stand and rolls her jeans up for a pillow.

Frankie Little Glynis? She's reserve team fodder, I'm back in the first as from today. I'm pulling Gantie's daughter tonight—Jacqueline.

Gillian No chance, Frankie. She's different class, you'll never make it.

Frankie I've got a five-pound-note with Roger Gilligan that says I will— you don't want to up it to a tenner, do you?

Gillian Be careful I don't take you up on that—I happen to know she's sitting down there with her mother.

Frankie You'd lose your wages, Gilly. Gantie's old woman's blown it out already. Nicked off home. Dear me, I'd have thought *you'd* have known that? The daughter's caning the bacardis and coke—the way she's putting them down in there she could be anybody's.

Gillian You still wouldn't do it, Frankie.

Frankie Why not?

Gillian Because if Jacqueline Gant was your intention, I'd be the last person on this earth you'd tell.

Frankie Why's that, then?

Gillian Because I'd tell Bernie.

Frankie You'd lose your wages again. I'd be double delighted if you did. If Gantie wants to fuck up my career, I'd like him to know that I can give his daughter even-stevens.

Gillian Is that how badly you want a transfer?

Frankie To be absolutely candid—yes.

Gillian It might get you away from the club, but you realize you'd leave your teeth behind? Bernie Gant would ram them down your throat.

Frankie Perhaps I'm big enough and old enough and man enough to clatter him.

Gillian I wouldn't bet your football boots on that, if I were you.

Frankie No—but it might make an interesting contest though—I'm conceding weight, but I must make favourite in years.

Gillian Do something for me, Frankie. Think about it first. Wait until Monday morning and ask him again about a transfer.

Frankie I've got the bird lined up in the Supporters' Club. I might not get the chance again.

Gillian And where's the great seduction scheduled to take place?

Frankie Her place or mine—who cares?

Gillian Hardly—you're in digs and she lives at home.

Frankie I'll find a place.

Gillian I thought you'd put the season ticket-holders' stand behind you when you knocked in both those goals.

Frankie There's always the Ringway Motel.

Gillian Always. As everybody knows. There always has been. It's a licensed knocking shop. And do you think you could get Jackie Gant to go there as long as she could stand? You'd have to carry *me*, to get me through the doors.

Frankie Where would you go?

Gillian If it was me that you were trying to make? Dinner at the Royal Hotel perhaps, then back to my flat.

Frankie Go on, you turned that down before the kick-off.

Gillian So try asking me again.

Frankie I never make application for the same fixture twice.

Gillian Don't you? I thought you were up here now for a transfer for the third time today?

Frankie I thought you put the block on a night out with me because you were sweating on a corruption of a minor charge?

Gillian You said yourself, Frankie, you moved up from the reserves into the first team squad today.

Frankie Are you serious?

Gillian It'll cost you a dinner at the Royal to find out—but it's a better-sounding bet than getting Jackie Gant pie-eyed and incapable.

Frankie What about Gantie? Aren't you supposed to be seeing him tonight?

Gillian No. I feel a bit like you, Frankie—sod Bernard Gant and sod football. Well?

Frankie I'm willing to give it serious consideration.

Gillian Don't take too long—it's an unrepeatable offer, it could easily get withdrawn.

Terence Bullivant enters, from the board-room, a drink in his hand

Terence Not you again? I had heard rumours you were unsettled on the playing staff—what are you after? A job on the office side?

Frankie No, Mr Bullivant. I just came up to have a word with Gillian.

Terence looks at them both in turn, surprised, considering the implications

Terence You're not waiting to see somebody?

Frankie No.

Terence Bugger off out of it then—you might have finished at twenty to five, but I've got work to do still.

Frankie (*to Gillian*) How long will you be?

Gillian I'm ready now. I've only got to put my coat on.

Frankie Five minutes' time then, in the players' bar. I'll ring the Royal and book a table.

Frankie moves to leave

Terence And Womersley?

Frankie Yes, Mr Bullivant?

Terence Congratulations on your game today, son. You played a blinder. I liked the way you took your second goal especially.

Frankie So did I.

Terence Very cool. I don't know why you want a move. You'll start next season here in the first team squad. Why ask for a transfer before you find out how much more you'll cop in your pay-packet if you stay with us?

Frankie I'm thinking things over this week-end. I'm going in to see the boss on Monday morning.

Terence That sounds more reasonable, Frankie, you do that thing—you give it some thought.

Frankie I will do, Terry.

Frankie goes out

Terence He's a cheeky young bugger, Womersley, but I have to admit it, he certainly turned it on today for us. Did I hear him mention something about booking a table at the Royal?

Gillian Did you?

Terence It certainly sounded to me as if I did.

Gillian Then you must have done.

Terence It's none of my business, I don't suppose, but has there been a minor upheaval in your private life?

Gillian You're right—it is none of your business.

Terence It's funny, Gillian, looking back, it seems like ages since you were were seen out and about, enjoying yourself, with one of the playing staff.

Gillian Does it?

Terence And yet I can put mind to a time when you were out gadding every night, with one or other of the lads, discothequing and that.

Gillian You get to grow out of discotheques. And that.

Terence Not at all. Nonsense. Enjoy yourself while you can. Get out and about with the younger end while you're young yourself. It does you good. It'll do young Womersley a bit of good to let some steam off after today's match. After you've had your meal, you want to get him to take you on somewhere.

Gillian What do you suggest?

Terence You'd know the answer to that better than me, Gillian. You know —somewhere for a nightcap. They do say the barman at the Ringway Motel has no great aversion to serving after time. Frankie's got a big decision to make by Monday. It might put him in the right frame of mind, so to speak, if things went right for him this week-end.

Gillian Excuse my ignorance if I've got hold of the wrong end of the stick, Mr Bullivant, but are you suggesting that I should go to bed with Frankie Womersley in order to keep him at the club? (*She takes her coat from the stand and starts to put it on*)

Terence No, of course I'm not—anyway, what the hell, I'm only suggesting you go out and have a good time and enjoy yourself, if it should come to the crunch—it's a bit late in the day, Gillian, for you to start thinking of it as a fate worse than bloody death.

By now Gillian has got her coat on, ready to leave

Bernie comes in; he also has a drink in his hand

Bernie You wanted a word in private, I think you said?

Terence Only because it's so noisy in the board-room you can't hear yourself think. Are you on your way then, Gillian?

Gillian Yes. (*To Bernie*) There was a message sent up from the Supporters' Club. Your wife's gone home. Your Jacqueline's still in there though. I believe she's drinking a bit more than she should. I believe something or somebody upset her earlier on. It's not her fault. I don't think you should leave her down there on her own too long. Oh, and by the way, your bottle of champagne is over there still, just where you left it. Oh yes—and Mr Bullivant, I hardly think it's likely, but if it does come to the crunch tonight—as you so delicately put it—I'll close my eyes and think of the F.A. Cup.

Gillian goes out

Bernie What was all that about?

Terence Haven't you heard, Bernie? It seems that our office lady has reverted to type. She's gone back on young players, would you believe? She's got herself fixed up tonight with Womersley. Dinner at the Royal Hotel, then on somewhere after that, discothequing and so forth. Mark you, there was a time, before you came to the club, when little Gilly was always putting it about, and then she seemed to quieten down— well, *I* haven't seen her around the town. Trust Frankie Womersley, the crafty dog. It's amazing what a couple of goals can do for you in the nooky stakes. I wish I was his age.

Bernie What was it you wanted a word about?

Terence Do you know, it's completely gone out of my head, so it couldn't have been all that important. Just a general chat, I suppose, about the direction in which we're going. You'll have gathered, from the atmosphere in the board-room, that the directors are behind you to a man?

Bernie I did hear certain opinions expressed.

Terence I'm not personally in agreement with a lot of the enthusiasms shown.

Bernie I had gathered that.

Terence You're a good coach. I'm not all that sure you're all that good a judge of a player. It's the most important thing at our level. We don't have the cash to buy established names. We have to rely on young lads we can raise from scratch.

Bernie I've some possibles and probables coming along. I've a lad in the Combination side who's going to be world class.

Terence The Nigerian? I'm not all that struck.

Bernie You weren't all that struck on Womersley before three o'clock.

Terence Point taken. I knew Womersley had got it, though—I also had him taped for an idle pig. You got him to run for you this afternoon— but can you get him to do it *every* Saturday afternoon all next season? Provided he even wants to stay?

Bernie He'll stay. And I shall do my best. You keep an eye on my little Nigerian, though. Watch how he strokes the ball now. That much potential I could sit and stare at him all week. He plays it sweet, and when football's sweet it's the best thing in the world. Give him two seasons and he'll get you promotion on his own.

Terence I haven't got two seasons. (*Nodding off to the board-room*) They're in there now, putting down the champagne and the double Scotches. They think we've worked a miracle because we've missed the drop, I think we're going to *need* a miracle next season to keep us out of another load of trouble.

Bernie Don't tell me—I start pre-season training in two months' time. Off we go again. Trying to get through to them as a team, trying to get through to them as individual players. Bullying kids and molly-coddling grown men—getting them to do more for you than you know they've got. I'm halfway between a sadist and a mother hen. So you steadily build them up, match-fit, then the kick-off comes and you watch them going down like nine-pins one by one, having lumps kicked off them. You want success, and somehow it seems harder every season. I've got two months. I want a midfield player, I want a right full-back, I need a goal-keeper as much as I'd like a million pounds in my back-pocket. I've a reserve team game on Monday, then on Tuesday we write this season off and it begins again for me—then. I shall be on the phone non-stop, chasing players who are on free transfers who might possibly have a bit of something somewhere no-one's noticed. I shall be ringing up managers who owe me favours, I shall be doing favours for managers in the hope that one day they'll do one for me. There's no such thing as the day the season ends—there's just the day you see the next season beginning.

Terence We're not entirely diametrically opposed. I want you to know that you will have my complete support next season.

Bernie Thanks.

Terence You're retained on the board's unanimous decision—I'm a paid servant of the club.

Bernie You and me both.

Terence For the sake of the club, you'll get my one hundred per cent backing.

Bernie That's what the club will get from me.

Terence That's what the club expects, next season. Good. (*Pause*) By the way, between these four walls, there's been a certain amount of—well—airing of views, shall we say—expressed by certain directors, regarding the chairman's capabilities. The structural organization of this club requires that the office of chairman be appointed by annual election, it's always——

Bernie For Christ's sake leave me out of board-room politics.

Terence I just wondered if you had any feelings one way or the other?

Bernie None whatsoever.

Terence Isn't that a rather negative approach?

Bernie Very probably. But then life's a sort of nil-nil draw. I'm a football manager. I'm one of a breed. I try to remain immune to feelings. I try to allow all needle and aggravation to have the same effect on me as water attempting to flow backwards up a duck's arse. Because if I didn't, Mr Secretary, I sometimes get the distinct impression that the double-dealing machinations and boot-licking intrigues of tin-pot, two-faced shit-pots such as you would eventually begin to wear me down.

A pause

Terence You'd better get the results next season, Gant, right from the bloody off, or by Christ you'll be out of work before the end of the pre-season matches before the season-proper starts.

Bernie Back on an even keel—I'd ten times rather have you for an enemy than on my side.

Terence And not just you, Gant. I'll see to it that that part-time scrubber that calls herself a full-time typist gets her marching orders too.

In a sudden burst of anger, Bernie grabs Terence by his coat lapels and lifts him off the ground

I'll call witnesses!

Bernie, in disgust, slings Terence across the room

Put one more hand on me and I'll see that you never work again in football.

Bernie Do that. Shout. Call who you like. Repeat in public what you've said to me and—stuff the job—I will, I'll break both your legs in half.

Another pause. Terence adjusts his tie, sourly

Do you know, I'm almost beginning to look forward to next season now.

Randolph bustles in

Here's the only man that really matters in this club. Without him it would cease to function. Randolph, do you ever stop fussing and fart-arsing around?

Randolph Very rarely, Mr Gant. But I've only got one phone call left to make today and that's me finished. As soon as I can remember where I put the phone book . . .

Randolph hunts for the phone directory. Bernie begins to get his things together: his overcoat; his champagne; some books and papers

Bernie That's it for me. (*He glances at his watch*) Is that all it is? A quarter to six? If I walk into the house at this time of night, the wife will think I'm after something. Especially with a bottle of champagne in my fist. I'm too old for them capers at my time of life.

Randolph You know what they say, Mr Gant.

Bernie That's football.

Randolph No, they say you're never too old to learn.

Harry Nicholls, full of drink and goodwill, pokes his head into the room

Harry Terence, come into the board-room, would you, and help me find that bottle of foreign firewater we fetched back from Yugoslavia on that tour. Bernie, don't say you're forsaking us? The booze-up's just beginning.

Bernie Not for me, Mr Chairman. I've an erring daughter to collect from the Supporters' Club.

Harry She can't come to any harm in there, surely to God? Still—you know best. (*Back to Terence*) Do you know which one I mean? That yellow stuff. Their chairman won't believe me when I say it's ninety-five per cent proof. I'm going to prove it to him. I'm going to drink it.

Terence goes out

Harry gives Bernie a double thumbs-up sign

Well done again, Mr Manager—here's to next season.

Harry returns a double thumbs-up sign himself

Bernie Here's to next season, Harry.

Harry goes out

Randolph, what the flaming hummers are you up to?

Randolph emerges from a cupboard, clutching a telephone directory

Randolph This is it. Only I've got to ring the undertakers.

Bernie Eh? I know that Womersley took some clog out there, but I didn't know he was that bad.

Randolph On behalf of Mr Harmsworth, deceased.

Bernie Who?

Randolph The late Vice-President of the Supporters' Club, Mr Gant, who had the sad misfortune to pass away before our triumph this afternoon. The reason why we wore black arm-bands. 'Course, it's come to light that he had nobody.

Bernie Didn't he?

Randolph Well, he'd been a widower for nearly thirty years. With him passing on the lot's come out. He had no kids, no relatives, he never even bothered with the neighbours. Do you know, he worshipped this club, he lived and breathed for it. I mean, I know it's your living and it's my passionate hobby, but it was his life. It was all he had. They found him dead in bed, you know. It was the police broke in because of all these milk bottles outside. He'd been lying there a couple of weeks—I thought he'd missed a game or two. They say his house was crammed with football magazines and programmes, stacked up in piles all round the walls. He loved this club. A true-blue fan—except we play in black and amber. The salt of the earth. Do you know what would have made him proud?

Bernie Surprise me?

Randolph If he could have only lived long enough to sit up in that stand, and see the lads in them black arm-bands, lined up inside the centre-circle, to commemorate his passing on.

Bernie No man can ask for more.

Randolph There's been a meeting convened by the committee in the Supporters' tea-room. They've passed a unanimous vote to give him a funeral service with full footballing honours. Will you excuse me, Mr Gant, one tiny moment? (*He dials a number*) Hello? Is that Capstick and Glazebrook's, funeral directors? . . . Ah, you won't know me personally, but I'm speaking on behalf of the football club. I believe a representative of ours has been on to you already, regarding the interment of our past Vice-President deceased? Do you still call it interment if it's a cremation? . . . I beg your pardon, Mr Glazebrook, I stand corrected. Anyway, I'm ringing you up regarding a slight technicality. The deceased had expressed a wish, apparently, to have his ashes

spread across our pitch. Hang on. There'd be no objections to that,
would there, Mr Gant, in principle?

Bernie I can't see any. They put ashes on roses, don't they? He'll be good
for the playing surface.

Randolph (*back into the telephone*) It doesn't create problems this end, if
it's all right at yours . . . His utmost wish, it's transpired . . . We have
a saying in our game, I don't know whether you've ever come across it?
That's football.

*Over the above, Bernie goes out, carrying his books, papers, bottle of
champagne, and giving Randolph a backward wave of his hand as he
goes*

CURTAIN

FURNITURE AND PROPERTY LIST

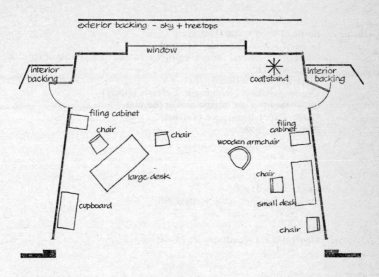

ACT I

On stage: Large desk. *On it:* telephone, writing materials, notebook, notepaper, envelopes, typing paper, carbons. *Beside it:* **Gillian**'s handbag with coins in purse

Small desk. *On it:* writing materials, files, books, papers

Cupboard. *In it:* football tickets, jug, bar of soap, various cups and glasses, telephone directory

2 filing cabinets. *On top of one:* pile of match programmes

Desk chair

3 small chairs

Wooden armchair

Coat-stand. *On it:* **Gillian**'s coat. **Bernie**'s coat.

Off stage: Battered tray with 3 cups of tea, 3 spoons, sugar-bowl **(Randolph)**

Glass of Scotch **(Harry)**

Glass of Scotch and soda **(Randolph)**

LIGHTING PLOT

ACT II

Off stage: Bottle of champagne **(Harry)**
            Glass of Scotch and soda **(Terence)**
            Glass of Scotch and soda, glass of vodka and tonic, bottle of light ale, glass **(Harry)**
            Black arm-bands **(Randolph)**
            Opened bottle of champagne, 2 glasses **(Harry)**
            Cardboard top hat, plastic beaker **(Bernie)**
            Glass of Scotch and soda **(Terence)**
Personal: **Bernie:** wristwatch

Property fittings required: nil
Interior. An office. The same scene throughout

ACT I.   Day
To open: General effect of autumn afternoon light
No cues

ACT II.   Day
To open: As Act I
No cues

EFFECTS PLOT

ACT I

Cue 1   **Randolph:** ". . . if not close friend."   (Page 1)
Telephone rings

Cue 2   **Gillian** picks up handbag   (Page 2)
Telephone rings

Cue 3   **Bernie:** ". . . buggering up the weather."   (Page 3)
Telephone rings

Cue 4   **Gillian:** ". . . otherwise engaged myself last night."   (Page 5)
Telephone rings

Cue 5   **Gillian:** ". . . my leisure-time activities."   (Page 5)
Telephone rings

Cue 6   **Randolph:** ". . . kicking and struggling."   (Page 7)
Telephone rings

Cue 7   **Frankie:** ". . . spelt my name wrong."   (Page 9)
Pause, then telephone rings

Cue 8   **Terence** exits   (Page 10)
Telephone rings

Cue 9   **Gillian:** ". . . where the chairman's got to."   (Page 12)
Pop music from loudspeakers on football field

Cue 10   **Bernie** closes window   (Page 12)
Cut off pop music

Cue 11   **Bernie** opens window   (Page 14)
Bring up pop music

Cue 12   **Bernie** closes window   (Page 14)
Cut off pop music

Cue 13   **Harry** opens window   (Page 16)
Bring up pop music

Cue 14   **Bernie** exits   (Page 17)
Fade pop music, bring up **Announcer's** *voice, cut off as* **Harry**
closes window

Cue 15   **Harry** opens window   (Page 19)
Bring up pop music, with crowd noises

Cue 16   **Terence:** ". . . to moan and jeer."   (Page 19)
Fade music—bring up sound of crowd chanting

Cue 17   **Terence** closes window   (Page 20)
Cut off crowd noises

Cue 18   **Harry** opens window   (Page 22)
Bring up crowd noises, louder—cut off when **Harry** *closes*
window

Cue 19	**Harry** opens window	(Page 25)
	Bring up crowd noises, still louder—cut off when **Harry** *closes window*	
Cue 20	**Terence:** "So it would appear, Gillian."	(Page 26)
	Sudden crowd roar, through closed window	
Cue 21	**Bernie:** ". . . it might rub off."	(Page 27)
	Repeat Cue 20	
Cue 22	**Randolph:** ". . . after we used them last time?"	(Page 30)
	Hymn—"Abide With Me"—from loudspeakers on football field	

ACT II

Cue 23	As CURTAIN rises	(Page 31)
	Crowd noises and referee's whistle, followed by pop music: cut off when **Gillian** *closes window*	
Cue 24	**Randolph:** ". . . Fourth Division material."	(Page 32)
	Telephone rings	
Cue 25	**Randolph:** ". . . that's bothering me."	(Page 32)
	Telephone rings	
Cue 26	**Randolph:** ". . . many of 'em—goals."	(Page 33)
	Chanting voices from football field—"Bernie Gant!" through closed window: bring up volume as **Harry** *opens window, cut off when he closes it*	
Cue 27	**Bernie:** ". . . put your bike away?"	(Page 37)
	Telephone rings	
Cue 28	**Gillian** ". . . in case it didn't work out."	(Page 39)
	Telephone rings	
Cue 29	**Gillian** picks up champagne bottle	(Page 47)
	Pause, then telephone rings	